The Art of
RISK &
REWARD

COMPILED BY
SHELLY YORGESEN

Edited by Eleanor Narey
Typeset by Dylan Ingram

 A catalogue record for this
work is available from the
NATIONAL National Library of Australia
LIBRARY
OF AUSTRALIA

National Library of Australia Catalogue-in-Publication data:
The Art of Risk and Reward/Shelly Yorgesen

ISBN:
978-0-6454663-1-7
(Paperback)

ISBN:
978-0-6454663-2-4
(Ebook)

PROLOGUE

I remember pausing early on in this journey, as I considered the risk of really putting myself out there. Fearing the public, would I actually do any good? Would what I envisioned to become be a blessing or a complete failure in the world?

As I relished in the good that is created when highly driven people collaborate, I decided I wanted to see what would happen if I started connecting business owners of the world.

… And so the book that you hold in our hands, *The Art of Risk and Reward,* is the physical evidence of worldwide collaboration.

This book had its book launch at Crom Castle in Northern Ireland on 6 May 2022. In formal gowns and suits we gathered in the presence of the Earl and Countess of Erne, in the library of their 300-year-old Castle. With men and women business owners who were once strangers now friends. Gathering from Australia, England, Northern Ireland, Canada, Scotland and the United States of America.

They have become friends through gathering together online every Wednesday, inside what we call Executive Networking Events Inner Circle, to open doors for each other, to share connections, to grow and scale their lives and businesses together.

Their stories are here: sharing their risk, their reward, the big gamble they took on themselves and how it turned out. Their efforts to make the world a better place. The day before the book launch, we had the beautiful opportunity to give them the stage in the conservatory of Crom Castle and hear them share their stories in person. They are incredible; I am so excited for you to read on.

The mountain range on the cover of this book is called the Grand Tetons. They aren't far from that fireplace in my living room where a little thought, a little dream, was hatched in my heart. A dream of creating a community that extends far beyond our little life in Idaho. They are known as the 'youngest' mountain range in the world.

To me, they signify all of us emerging from the ground, the newest in our families to take the risks that we have taken. Pushing rock against rock, moulding the future from the efforts of our work.

Last Christmas, our global network hosted Christmas in six countries. Through our non-profit, Operation Christmas Magic, we have stashed all around the world Santas and Mrs Clauses, bringing what we call a 'grand surprise' to hearts that hurt. From Honduras to West Africa, to Guatemala, to Uganda, from Idaho to Kenya …

… And so, from the farm to the castle, to a little home in Uganda, the art of the risk, of stepping out into a global community, is absolutely worth the reward.

CONTENTS

NETWORKING IN THE LARGEST COUNTRY IN THE WORLD

SHELLY YORGESEN

As we drove up to the castle, I tried to keep myself in check, but the tears fell without my permission. It had been nearly two years of planning, two years of meetings, two years of marketing, two years of learning …

… And here we finally were.

As we drove up the driveway, the castle seemed to just grow out of the gorgeous green landscape that surrounds it; it seemed as if I was in a dream, and then I heard a member of our team say, 'Shelly, are you okay? Are you crying?'

… And indeed, I was.

I had decided to take what I loved into the world, with no real skills that fit the task. I wanted to conquer the world of the online space, I wanted to build membership, I wanted to gather business owners from every corner of the globe.

The funny thing is, this is not where I started …

I was working in my yard one day, barefoot, like I love to garden, feeling the warm moist dirt between my toes, really connecting with nature and this beautiful planet God gave us to enjoy.

… When a thought came to mind, that wasn't my own.

'Your next product is you.'

I think I had a wheelbarrow in my hands, and I stopped dead in my tracks. I have worked to be prayerful and in tune with heaven for many years, I knew this was not my thought, but I had no idea what I was going to do with it.

A few days later, a business conference came through my social feed, I was at the time contracted as an executive director for a local company. We also were in full operation with moving produce from three states into five states under our brand Farm Fresh Fundraisers. I decided I need to learn what that voice was talking about, so I booked a plane ticket and a hotel, and very, very unlike me, I went alone.

I took my journal, my open heart, zero expectations and that memory of the voice that barefooted day. I was about to create our future.

By the time the garden shovels, wheelbarrows and summer season had passed, and winter was in full swing, another business post crossed my feed. I remember it perfectly, it was January 2016, I was laying on the carpet in my living room late in the evening in Idaho. Our fireplace was warm and roaring.

I learned from that article something that blew my mind. For the first time in my life, I was learning that I could market a product in the online space, a product from my knowledge, from my experience, that would be for sale 24/7!

… Now, the fall between the wheelbarrow and the fireplace had been full of me orchestrating semi-truck after semi-truck of our potatoes, apples and oranges all across Utah, Idaho, Washington, Wyoming and California.

The idea that I could make money without the liability of semi-trucks, of youth selling our produce, of forklifts unloading produce, all blew my mind. I remember pausing on my phone, reading and rereading the text. I told my sweetheart about it, we talked about it for a few days, and then finally we decided to invest our first-ever $997 in an online course. My first ever.

Bret and I would talk for hours about what our product would be, about what that voice in the yard was talking about. We hammered through day after day, conversation after conversation, what was it that I was to add to the world, and how could we work at it together.

Bret has worked as a chemical engineer for twenty years with the same company, they decommission all aircraft carriers and nuclear submarine fuel for the US Navy here in Idaho (Idaho is way more than just potatoes!). We had worked together in several side-hustles over the years, and we knew there was something bigger coming.

Yes, we took the potato money, that original $997, and added the equivalent of the cost of a graduate degree from an Ivy League school for me to acquire the knowledge and skills it took to build a globally recognised company. Executive Networking Events (ENE) now has an international online membership and following with over 7,000 business owners from nearly every country in the world.

Sitting next to me in that van in front of the castle was my sweetheart Bret, our oldest daughter Brooke and Karen Mc Dermott. The world-renowned author and publisher of this book and my two other books. It was her and me, and Jordelle our event director and member director that had been meeting weekly for nearly two years to put this castle mastermind together.

I walked up to the front door of Crom Castle, the beautifully aged, extra-large doorknob turned, and there he was, open arms and a big smile ready to greet us. It was the Seventh Earl Erne, John Crichton. His lovely bride of just a few months had spent the weekend before our arrival scouring the property for fresh flowers and had a gorgeous bouquet in every room.

Our castle ticket holders began to arrive, 11 flew in from Idaho, some from Australia, Canada, France, Ireland, China and Northern Ireland. When the goal is connection and collaboration, and I was the host, you tend to take a moment and look around into the faces of all of the ticket holders and wonder what conversations and connections will they make, what ideas will they have, what good this will do for them and their businesses, their families and their future.

They had invested their time and their money to attend, they had flown, in some cases, all the way across the world. I took their success very personally, and I have to admit that I wished I had a little time machine to make a quick trip into the future to see how their investment in this week in a castle would affect their life.

The week proceeded ahead perfectly, we hosted two professionally choreographed executive networking events: one on Tuesday, one on Thursday. Local business owners converged on the castle to meet and network with the attendees from eight countries.

On Wednesday of the event, I was sitting next to Karen in the drawing room, and Ron Malhotra was sharing a very interesting story of how the mind works and how we can use our minds powerfully to help us get what we seek most.

Karen had picked up her phone to respond to a message that

had just come in. I had kicked off my heels for the day, and my lucky yellow event shoes (my yellow Converse) were also on the floor in front of us.

I leaned over and asked, 'Hey, Karen, what are you doing?'

'Closing a deal with the Duchess of York,' she said with a smile.

I turned to her and said, 'Let's soak in this moment, together, you and I, mothers to eleven children, who live on two different continents, you in Australia and me in the US. You became a member of my global networking community to break into an American market as a publisher. You came up with this idea to host an event together in a castle, we sold tickets, rented a castle, it's the first business event of its kind in Crom Castle in 300 years … and here you sit, closing a deal with the Duchess of York!'

We both smiled; smiles of gratitude for the journey, smiles of gratitude for the courage, smiles of gratitude for the future not only for us, but also for all who had taken a chance on us to attend and were sitting in the room with us.

The magical week at Crom Castle unfolded even bigger and better than we ever dreamt. Alliances were made, deals were done, and now three years later as I write this, I just got word that one of the attendees', Heather Burgett, total earnings from those relationships built in those castle walls has now reached $100,000!

We had taken a risk on hiring a speaker for the event, his name is Christopher Kai. *Inc.* Magazine calls him the 'Billionaire Networker'. Also, three years after the Castle, he and I hosted an event together. Actually three events, at the first one we made $87,000 together.

Heather said it well, 'The Crom Castle mastermind is the gift that keeps on giving!'

Now, I can't end my chapter here without also sharing that as we ended the event, there was not one but TWO marriage proposals! One planned, one spontaneous!

It all happened the night of the formal gala, presented by the Earl and Countess of Erne. After a full week of adventure, connections and memories made, we were led into the grand dining room by a bagpiper.

A few weeks ahead of the event, one of the attendees, Trever Gerdes, had reached out to me to see if we would let him repropose to his sweetheart of twenty-five years, he said he had done a terrible job the first time, and he wanted to do it again.

To her complete surprise, he took a knee right there during the gala and gave her a beautiful blue ring to match her incredible blue gown.

… Then a surprise.

James Billman, a cowboy, restaurant owner, real estate hotshot asked me for the microphone. Now, I know James well, his big mischievous smile, giving him the microphone is risky business! … But you bet.

He also took a knee and proposed! He and Melisa had been dating and came together to the castle, she also said yes!

What a way to end a very magical week. Those business meetings that I had flown to were nothing compared to what had happened at our business event!

Today the magic continues, we are nearly three years past this amazing week, this book you are reading is set for its book launch in the library of Crom Castle on 6 May 2022 at our second Crom Castle mastermind.

We have a global membership of business owners and executives, we host monthly virtual events and annual fancy global events at the castle and more. We are teaching them to build their own profitable communities online, using the power of Facebook to network. Helping them build large followings of their own to serve the world and build connections.

That day in my garden, barefoot and open-hearted, I never would have thought that a farm girl and a farm boy, who met in high school, fell in love, had five children, raised in small-town USA would have taken the journey to connect the world as we have.

There will be days when you feel something, when a little voice prompts you to act, don't doubt it, just act, you may end up renting a castle because you listened …

SHELLY YORGESEN

Executive Networking Events (ENE)
Idaho, USA

Shelly Yorgesen is the founder and CEO of Executive Networking Events (ENE), a global pioneer in high-level executive connections and communities. Whether through high-ticket exclusive masterminds at a 1,900-acre estate in Ireland or in online communities, she has successfully helped thousands of entrepreneurs and executives understand how to create and leverage their networks to grow their businesses. Shelly is also an international speaker, bestselling author, and the co-founder and president of Operation Christmas Magic, an Idaho-based non-profit which creates and curates bespoke charity events for her local and global community.

RISK AND THE GOD OF RECOMPENSE

MELODY DAWES

It would be a lie if I described the reward of all that has come my way if I did not mention the hand of the Lord God Almighty in my life.

My life is a series of risks taken. Honestly, I don't even know another way to approach life. Has every risk been rewarded? Absolutely not. However, every risk has been answered – if not with the reward, then with the lesson learned, the new relationship made, or even the experience marked off.

One of the first risks I remember was when I was 15 and deciding upon some electives to take as I entered my sophomore year of high school. My best friends were all choosing classes that did not appeal to me, and my daddy suggested I take speech. I really did not know what the class would cover, but my father assured me that, even if I never gave a formal speech in my life, I would always need to know how to present myself in a public setting. I was a solid student and did well in school, but I was never comfortable giving oral reports or being in front of people.

That class changed so much about me! I learned how to give a substantial talk within a seven-minute time frame. I learned how to quickly pull together a speech in a competitive situation. And I learned how to stand up in front of a crowd at the last moment and give an impromptu presentation that had enough value to keep my audience engaged. I also learned that doing something new and different was fun!

The reward? Self-confidence, critical thinking skills, over-coming the fear of speaking and learning how to be perpetually prepared, to name a few. As an adult, I have drawn upon those classes over and over and never would have dreamed that I would use that skill to speak to numerous classes and audiences of all sizes through the years.

I took another risk in 2006 at the age of 52. I purchased a local magazine with no solid business experience, a little bit of writing and editing experience, and a bucket full of enthusiasm willing to learn.

I had been a preacher's wife my entire adult life and had helped my husband start a publishing company on the side. I had also been writing a column called 'Musings from Melody' for a few years that was published in several area newspapers in our region of Texas.

This family magazine was a monthly publication that was dis-tributed FREE in hospital lobbies, clinics, day cares, restaurants and other places where families gathered. The magazine was supported by family-friendly local businesses and already had a healthy reputation even though it was only a ten-year-old busi-ness. I LOVED working in this industry and quickly made many connections as well as friends throughout our city as I sold ads, sourced family events to share with my readers and provided helpful information to parents raising their children and building a solid home life.

We took quite a risk in this venture. My husband believed enough in my abilities to risk our finances for the purchase, and I believed that my determination to continue to grow this publication would be met with not only financial success, but a sense of purpose and meaning that fit into the legacy I intended to leave in the world.

In 2012, my husband, who pastored, owned a book publishing company and was a speaker at multiple retreats, died suddenly late one night. I mention this because he died on the eve of the day all of the work that I put into the magazine was to be submitted to my graphic designer for the final layout. I did not have everything completed and ready to send, but I did have an awesome graphic designer, a precious friend who could edit the few remaining articles and a son who stayed on the phone with both of them the next day to make sure they had all they needed to complete their tasks. That magazine was sent to the printer on time and hit the stands on time while most of my 30,000 readers never knew that my husband had died and a service for him had been performed the previous week.

At that moment, I began to realize the importance of having a system in place that could keep rolling even when I could not perform. I realized the value of having a team around me that understood my vision, my goals and my platform to continue the work even when I was unavailable.

After a couple of years of living life alone and working many hours keeping my husband's publishing business going as well as my magazine, I was growing weary and decided I wanted to sell the magazine. I came across a young entrepreneur in Lubbock who had just begun a wedding magazine. Being in his twenties and full of hope for his future, he had his eyes set on growing a grand publishing empire. He was interested in purchasing my magazine, but did not have the available cash. He brought an offer to me that included becoming my partner in the family magazine, changing the format to a quarterly and agreeing that after partnering for one year, he would then be able to complete the purchase and I could retire. Little did I know at the time, that what looked like a great solution was actually the biggest risk yet that I was to take in my business endeavors.

The details do not really matter; however, the short version is, he lied to some of my faithful advertisers, he embezzled funds from our business account and he took advantage of the close friendship we had developed within our partnership and betrayed the trust. This all happened within about an 18-month period of time. Upon discovering this hard truth and upon the recommendation of my lawyer, he left the company, I ended up taking his wedding magazine to cover the cost of the funds he stole. I also then needed to quickly repair some business relationships.

I remember lying in bed one night thinking through every detail of what had occurred and realizing that the partnership that was supposed to lead to the sale of the magazine and retirement, had now brought me a magazine with advertisers that had been disappointed, fewer funds in my account and more weariness now than when the partnership had begun. That risk-filled decision did NOT work out well for me. But, I knew that the God who had been with me all my life was watching over this event as well. As I lay in bed, the word 'recompense' came to my mind. That was a word I rarely heard or used, but I couldn't get it out of my mind. I got up out of bed and checked the actual definition as well as looked up how God used the word in the Bible. While the word is not common, it did show up in ways that assured me that God would bring recompense (meaning to make amends for a loss or harmful situation).

I recently sold the publishing company I have built over the last 16 years for a nice little sum – we could even call it the reward of recompense. How did that happen? Well, first of all – with God's guidance.

He showed me how to gain back the trust of those advertisers. He showed me how to increase the visibility of both magazines. He showed me how to cut the costs and increase the profit. He showed me how to reduce the staff and still handle the workload.

Did this all happen overnight? Absolutely not. However, day by day, business increased. Little by little, both of the magazines recovered and even began to prosper quicker than I could have imagined. I sought out business leaders to help grow my net-work and realized that there were more opportunities available for success and growth, than the hardships that I almost allowed to overtake me.

In the last couple of years, I moved to another beautiful Texas town, Weatherford, to be closer to my children. I have learned how to work my business completely remotely, and I have built a new home and literally just moved in.

Because God's hand has been so strongly shown in this, I will end with one of the scriptures that carried me through much of the past few years. This is from the book of Ruth and found in chapter 2, verse 12.

'May the LORD bring recompense to you for what you have done. May you be richly rewarded by the LORD, the God of Israel, under whose wings you have come to take refuge.'

MELODY DAWES

MKD Publishing
Weatherford, TX

Melody has owned MKD Publishing company for 16 years, starting with *Lubbock's Home & Family Magazine*. She later added *Weddings by Wendy Rose* and also published a few books for local authors. Melody recently sold both magazines and is currently laying the foundation to help baby boomers write the highlights of their life stories to pass on to future generations.

Her book, *Kisses To Grow On*, is a compilation of essays written over a two-year period of time that were published in a number of area newspapers. The book is filled with sentimental, yet humorous, stories on raising children, and continues to bless parents today.

Besides her passions of reading and writing, Melody loves the sport of pickleball and tries to play three to four times a week. She has also found the tournament circuit for senior amateurs and already entered a few with her eye on entering at least six a year.

Melody was married to Don for almost 39 years and is the mother of Rachel, Rebekah and Marcus. Her children are all grown and married, as well as living out their lives according to the risks in front of them. She has 12 grandchildren from the ages of ten to 21 and loves to watch them perform, play, excel, fail, get up and go again. Her life dream is to watch each of her children and grandchildren fulfill their God-given mission in life and be a blessing to the part of the world they live in.

Above all, Melody loves to build personal relationships with the people she meets and counts it a thrill to be able to enjoy such diversity in her life. Her loyalty as a friend is built on laughing until someone is crying, crying until someone is laughing, and appreciating the moments of adventure as well as the moments of stillness.

While none of us knows how many days we have left on this earth, Melody has determined that every day she will attempt to bring a blessing in some form to someone.

Contact: melody@mkdpublishing.com

PANDEMIC, PANIC AND THE POTATO GIRL

JONATHAN CLARK

Diary entry 17 February 2022 ENE member Bertie Le Roux: 'If I may say you're like a different person to who you were six months ago ...'

Ever since the internet hit the UK in 2000, I wanted the internet lifestyle – working from my laptop, able to work anywhere, with a global business. Today I get up at 7:45 am, make a tea to go and take our son Luke to school. I drive home listening to inspirational audiobooks and sit down to plan 'my day my way'. Zoom appointments start around noon, mostly with USA or Canada. The pandemic built the habit of a daily walk, so my wife Cheryl and I usually go to a nearby park, then back for lunch. I live stream in the afternoon, then one of us collects our son from school and comes back for tea and a family catch-up, then back to business. Dinner is a pleasure with the family and usually followed by Netflix or a good movie. Back to working on my next Amazon novel, then training with my Accelerate Coaches before bed.

But it wasn't always this good. My wife's health issues mean she'll never work again, so I'm the sole breadwinner. In 1997 I launched my NLP and hypnotherapy practice and managed to grow to six figures a year, jetting off to Hawaii every six months and life was good. Unfortunately, the 2008 recession strangled that business. Nobody wanted NLP anymore. My skill set was storytelling, training and building a practice. I had 17 online courses ready, but would anyone buy them? For the first time, I was full of fear and doubt. My boyish enthusiasm had been replaced by cynicism.

Luckily every business needed to get online, and I'd already done it for myself – so in 2008 Instant Edge was born, a marketing agency for small businesses. A 'done for you' service, I would meet with the client to get what we needed, then we would create online videos, social media, websites, emails and book launches. Every new client was like me starting a new business. I couldn't do it alone so I built a team of nine freelancers.

By February 2020 I was fed up living in the car, the parking fees, stress, traffic and missing time with Luke. Attending face-to-face networking events with the same old faces going nowhere fast, convinced me I needed to find a better group. I told Cheryl, 'There has to be a better way than this!'

A month later came lockdown. Everything was on Zoom. Then it got weird: clients got tetchy, started to have unrealistic expectations and became argumentative, demanding that we did more than we agreed. Paying us to do stuff they didn't want to do, then criticizing the work. We doubled a CBD company's sales, then they sacked us. I lost it with one client who changed his book cover 17 times! There were refunds, harsh emails and one client even threatened me.

Several were so desperate for money that they stopped paying.

Five of my friends and colleagues died in six months. I was burned out being ruled by client demands and pandemic uncertainty. Networking went virtual but attendance was low and morale even lower. Four of my team caught COVID-19 or decided to let the government pay them to stay at home and not work. My workload doubled. Truth is, I resented the clients and hated my business. Cheryl hated it more and that caused so many arguments. Every morning I woke up with 'The Fear', scared to open my email.

That's when ENE appeared. A new global networking group with 6,000 members. They were upbeat, fun, hungry, high energy, collaborative. The opposite of the Scottish networking crowd – downbeat, downtrodden, tired, desperate. ENE was alive, refreshing. On 24 May 2021, I joined the ENE free Facebook group.

Diary entry 30 May 2021: I saw a man acting suspiciously across the street, so I went over to investigate. I saw what I thought was a kid stuck up a tree. Actually, a young man trying to hang himself! I called the police while Cheryl kept him talking until they arrived to cut him down. If I hadn't gone over there, he'd be dead. Things were bad but not that bad.

On 9 June I booked the next ENE networking event. Unfortunately, I wouldn't make it …

Diary entry 12 June: Incinerated old client files, blessing them and asking God to clear any blocks.

Diary entry 15 June 2021: The morning started normally in the shower, thought maybe I had pulled a muscle, there was a slight twinge below my ribs which got progressively more painful, and soon I was vomiting in the bathroom. Within minutes I was doubled over in pain on the floor and I begged Cheryl to call a doctor. He sent us straight to the hospital. I got a nice cuddle from

Luke and I was painfully aware that I was scaring him. I drew a heart on his car window as I didn't know when I'd see him next. I was in acute receiving with a suspected kidney stone during a global pandemic. I was fit as a flea and I hadn't been in hospital in 35 years. What the hell? What if I caught COVID-19?

Seven days of torture followed. Every four hours I got an injection into my stomach, I was on a drip and I cycled between searing agony in my side, spaced-out on opiates or exhausted sleep. Mercifully the doctors decided not to operate or insert a camera somewhere you shouldn't insert anything, but instead wait for it to pass naturally. Easy for them to say! All the while I was worrying about not earning, *What if I can't work, what if they have to operate and I'm off for a month? Will Cheryl cope?*

Who'll tell my clients? One client relentlessly hounded me by phone and text while I was in there!

I'd never prayed before, but in that hospital, I prayed daily, and I still do. I had a lot of time to think about the future, maybe even a new business. On 18 June I was lying in my hospital bed and got a lovely voice message from Shelly Yorgesen, CEO of ENE. That meant a lot.

Diary entry 22 June 2021: The 4 mm stone squeezed through a 2 mm tube millimeter by agonizing millimeter and came out. I was discharged that afternoon, and we were sitting on the decking enjoying the fresh air and sunlight when Shelly called to see how I was. It took a week to catch up with the avalanche that was waiting for me at my desk.

On 2 July I decided to join the ENE Inner Circle – quality people, high caliber. One resource Shelly provided was the full ENE business model. It took 90 minutes to set it up. A week later I had three Zoom calls and signed up all three clients, within a week I'd earned four figures from a Facebook group. Could I risk closing down the old agency and doing this instead?

On 10 August I shared the full story with Shelly, who'd called me personally, and I was flattered that she'd do that. She's walking her dogs in Idaho and I'm looking out the window in Glasgow at the trees, and I can still see the blue rope the police cut through lying on the ground.

18 August and I'm in ENE's 'Million Dollar Think Tank', struggling to hold it together. Money was still tight and my mother had fallen and suffered a brain bleed. I was perched on the end of her bed during the call while ambulance drivers wheel-chaired her into the other room. I could barely hold back the tears and stress of two hellish months. But the support the ENE guys showed me was amazing.

In October I shot a testimonial video for ENE – I'd never seen a mentor pull back the curtain like the Wizard of Oz, and hand you their exact business model. Growing my groups while winding down the old clients, relieved to get each one completed.

Shelly then launched her accelerate program. A weekly one-hour live stream where I do my thing – training and storytelling, and the perfect home for my online courses.

Which brings us back to today. Do you believe in omens? I do … The young man trying to hang himself.

Praying for all blocks to be cleared.

The week in hospital reassessing things.

An angel called Shelly showing up at exactly the right time.

A bigger and better global networking group.

Accelerate the perfect business model.

ENE (especially Shelly) gave me the hope and focus to fight 'The Fear' with everything I had, and the vehicle I needed. Today

I'm happier, healthier, I've got my mojo back and I'm loving helping people grow a business that they love as much as I love mine. I took a risk, and there have been so many rewards. Thank you, Potato Girl.

JONATHAN CLARK

Instant Edge
Glasgow, Scotland

Jonathan Clark is a six-time bestselling author who helps thought leaders (authors, experts, coaches, consultants and speakers) who want to build a loyal tribe of fans who buy their stuff by showing them how to build a business with five streams of income in the next six months.

He has been described as 'Sir Alan Sugar meets Peter Pan'. He started his first business in 1985 at age 18 and now teaches step-by-step strategies that act like treasure maps to help thought leaders get more leads, close more deals and take more time off.

His 'Get Found, Get Hired, Get Paid' program not only shows you how to build all of this, but he does it WITH YOU so you actually get them done! By the end of the six months, you have a bestselling book published on Amazon Kindle and in paperback, a signature talk with slides ready to present, your own online course for sale, a coaching wing for 1:1 or groups, and a consulting wing for corporate work.

His work has been featured in the *Daily Mail*, *The Fred Macaulay Show*, *STV 2*, *Radio Clyde*, *BBC Radio Scotland*, *The Sunday Post*, and *The Glasgow Herald*. Previous clients have included three finalists on *Dragons' Den*, Virgin Cinemas, sporting professionals and Papa John's Pizza.

He increased Morgan Stanley's sales by 40% within 30 days, has trained Barclays' sales trainers in NLP techniques and has lectured twice at the Peter Jones Entrepreneur Academy. A regular speaker at the Hunter Centre for Entrepreneurship at Strathclyde University, Jonathan has racked up over 5,000 hours of one-to-one consultations and is often hired as a keynote speaker.

Jonathan lives in Glasgow with his wife and son, and when he's not helping people simplify their marketing, he likes playing loud guitar, playing with his son and generally just playing.

He is passionate about what he does and he loves to help his clients make more money and enjoy the lifestyle they want for themselves and their families. You can reach him on +44 141 639 7099 or email admin@instantedge.co.uk, or JOIN OUR FREE FACEBOOK GROUP at www.foundhiredpaid.com

Contact: admin@instantedge.co.uk

CHALLENGING THE STATUS QUO

PEGGY NILES

It's not always the easiest or the straightest path that gets you where you want to go; sometimes you have to be willing to challenge the status quo!

It was back in 2001, I found a lump in my breast and spent a good part of four or five months going back and forth with exams to see if I had to deal with one of the hardest struggles. As I was getting close to finally receiving a determination, 9/11 hit. I worked in Sears Tower at the time (although that morning I was at a client's office nearby in downtown Chicago), I had two young sons, my husband was also working downtown, and like every other American in the country, I watched in horror the devastation that hit our country.

Downtown Chicago was a mere panic ground; as I walked down the street I could feel the tension, the fear, the disbelief. The media was saying Sears Tower was evacuated when I knew it was a lie – I had coworkers and friends still working inside.

I called my husband and told him I was on my way to the

train station and to please get out when he informed me there was no way in hell we should both be in Union Station at the same time. Afterall, we had two young sons at home and Union Station (like Sears Tower) was a potential target.

Reality two set in for me.

I hailed one of the few cabs available, had the driver get on the expressway headed toward our suburb, called my husband again and said, 'Okay, now get the hell out of there!'

When I got home the house was empty, I turned on the TV where I became glued and watched in dismay, tears unconsciously running down my cheeks.

It was that day I realized we truly can die at any time – totally outside of our control.

Fear, anger, patriotism, strength – so many emotions.

After all of that settled down I questioned myself, 'Why am I doing this? Why am I working so hard to help some rich people get richer?' Life is too short and too valuable.

It was shortly after that I started re-evaluating how I lived, how I worked, who I worked for – my choices.

It was at that moment I started thinking of a plan to change things I did have control over. I knew, though, I wasn't quite ready to go on my own; there were still a few things I needed to learn.

I took on extra projects at work outside of my realm. Now my goal was to gain as much experience in business before I could properly serve my own clients, formal process management (or re-engineering) was something I still wanted to solidify.

I took on a role where I was a regional senior manager responsible for three regions, two of which were mainly virtual. I basically had three partners I reported to, one of which was old-school and didn't like having someone in my role that worked on a flexible work arrangement – that is, reduced hours and partially virtual.

I successfully improved client satisfaction, empowered team members, improved profits by 33% within seven months, and launched two national projects: process re-engineering for our national team and outsourcing of work to India.

Despite being successful, it was not good enough for the old-school partner. Every three to six months or so, he would insist upon bringing a male counterpart in to replace me. Each time the other two partners gave in and moved me to another section. Each time, the other senior manager would fail and they would bring me back in to keep things going.

At long last, the firm decided nationally to go through major lay-offs in all areas. It was my charge to lay-off many members of my local team; after I completed that miserable task, it was my turn.

The two supportive partners I reported to assumed I would fight it because that was my nature: optimistic, proactive and persistent. They asked what I wanted to do. They asked if I wanted to be reassigned within the firm. 'I'm done,' was my response. 'I'm tired of fighting something that will never change. Despite me proving over and over again how successful this has been, this vicious circle will not end and I'm not going to continue to play the game.'

My choice now was do I go to work for another firm or start my own company?

I had no doubt I could get another job in a similar position at another firm, paid health insurance for my family, guaranteed six-figures and a flexible work arrangement. I was, however, tired of making money for people who didn't appreciate it, or me.

Throughout my life, so many friends, coworkers and acquaintances told me, 'I wish I could ...' or 'If I did ...' but they never followed through. I wanted to help the average person follow through; I wanted to help them go after their 'what-ifs'.

In reality, I'll admit it, I always seemed to fight for the underdog: challenging the way things were done, proving I could lead a team and be successful managing the workload and processes even if I worked less hours or worked out of the office for a portion of the week. In my mind I wasn't doing it just for myself, I was doing it for those behind me that wanted to have a career and a life without having to choose between the two.

On the home front I had two young boys under the age of eight and my husband was a self-employed consultant in the process of purchasing a company.

Risk or security?

As I sat on the beach of Boca Raton, Florida (attending a firm management conference no less), my decision came to me. I was ready – it was time to go out on my own. Things happen for a reason, and to me, the timing meant it was time to make my dream a reality.

I wasn't really worried. Every time I set a goal for myself and went after what I wanted, I got it. Was it easy? No, of course not, but I would figure out what needed to be done to get where I wanted, plan it out and do it!

I remember starting out; I remembered things from my marketing classes in college as if I had applied them for years. I even made cold calls. I remember my husband saying, 'Good for you. I could never do that.' My response was, 'What's the worst that happens, they say no? I'd be no worse off than I am right now.'

I went to networking events where one head of a networking

organization responded saying how boring my work was. Didn't let it phase me; in fact, I laughed it off.

I understood what I did wasn't appealing to most people, all of my career I was considered 'overhead'.

Here's the thing, it may not have sounded sexy, but the results I could get were undeniable. I'll actually go as far as to say a necessity.

Within a year I was making more than I made at my last job and working even less hours. I attended every baseball and hockey practice of my sons, went on trips with the teams for out-of-town games and tournaments, was room-mom for school, all while running my business.

Within a couple years I was making what would have taken me seven to ten years to make had I stayed employed by someone else. Again, I knew I had a ton of experience in the core aspects of running a business, but I really wanted to help others achieve more success as well.

At first I labeled myself as an accounting firm, but years later my youngest son helped me realize I was doing so much more for my clients when I took him with me to meet a client. I wasn't just advising them on their accounting, but also on growing their overall business. Deep down my real goal was to help make dreams a reality!

In the back of my mind, I remembered my first boss out of college would get mad when I'd ask him questions. He would say, 'Stop asking me questions and just do what I say.' Well, that didn't sit well with me; how could I learn if I didn't ask questions? So I kept asking – I kept learning – I kept trying to improve!

I found two of the most important questions are 'Why?' and 'How?'. Why are we doing this? Why are we getting these results? How can we do things differently? How can we make this more effective?

I worked daily ... dialing in my framework until it was sustainable, running a company from a strategic-based approach that changes lives while at the same time changing your bottom line ($$$).

So, what I was doing was looking at CEOs and business owners and I started helping and consulting with them.

I started observing their almost addictive behavior to working harder and not smarter, but then I started realizing it wasn't really their fault.

It was confusing trying to figure out what to work on first and they were often managing difficult employees – in some situations declining profits.

They had to be in 100 places at once, and the worst part about it was they felt like they were the only people who could really manage it all because it was all on their shoulders, the expertise lied with them.

They didn't really have anybody else to help them and that's when I started really digging deep, diving into research, looking into articles, hundreds of hours studying what they should be focusing on.

I discovered three key leverage points, kind of indicators ... I found, with a little bit of focus, even each day, looking at these leverage points, they started developing a systematic plan and just like a little tiny lever point can move an entire object (like a fulcrum can move an entire seesaw), these three leverage points became catalysts for their entire businesses.

Not only did their profits start soaring, but here's the crazy part, they started gaining back ten to 20 hours in the work week. So they were gaining hours back, they were working less.

But it didn't just stop with that; they also started enjoying the culture at work because their employees were happier, profits were doing great and one of the side benefits I saw with the CEOs and executives was they stopped thinking that they hired wrong or their team members were incompetent.

This just caused an even more empowering culture inside of their organization.

You see, for me, it's more of a strategic game or mystery that I thrive on ... looking for the hidden opportunities for my clients, figuring out what pieces are missing to catapult their businesses forward faster, but most of all helping business owners live life on their terms!

I found the greatest reward for myself, and my clients, is having more control over our lives, our choices.

The flexibility to spend time with my family when I wanted and show up for all my kids' activities, the ability to choose who I worked with and how I did things, the ability to work from home, a beach, my grandmother's cottage – wherever I wanted, the capability to take my dad to his cancer treatments and be by his side that last month; these were the things I cherished.

Making more money while working less hours; these were the things that made me feel fortunate.

Helping clients gain more flexibility and freedom to realize their dreams; these are the things that made me feel fulfilled.

Just as there were things out of my control when 9/11 hit in 2001, there are things outside my control today. The difference is that I have since focused on things I *can* control and by doing so, by challenging the status quo, I am able to live life on my terms – the reward far outweighs the risk!

PEGGY NILES

Quantum Scaling^{SM}

Illinois, USA

Peggy Niles' passion is to help overworked business owners live their dream lifestyles while using their business to make their mark or impact on the world. She is the owner and performance and profit strategist of Quantum Scaling.

Peggy has worked with Hyatt Corporation, Alberto-Culver International, Ernst & Young and other large corporations; advised on mergers and acquisitions for companies ranging from six to nine figures; and worked with small-business owners to scale their companies profitably. Like most of her clients, her story started with trying to gain flexibility and freedom without choosing between a career and enjoying life. After 17 years in the corporate and public accounting world, Peggy figured out how to lead a team and get things done in half the time while taking Fridays off, even in a virtual environment. She now uses her Profitable Exit Framework with business leaders to challenge the status quo and avoid doing things the same way because that's how it's always been done. Leveraging numbers, processes and on-point actionable strategies, these owners live life on their terms as they grow, scale their companies and position themselves for a profitable exit. Working with Peggy allows leaders to have control over their business without being intimately involved with every aspect. They learn to make their own choices with predictability instead of reacting to the issues of the day. They become leaders running a business instead of employees of a company they own. To learn more about Quantum Scaling or get help with your business, email info@anbconcepts.com or join our Facebook group: facebook.com/groups/ProfitwithStrategy. Check out our website www.strategicscalingsolutions.com.

Contact: pniles@quantumscalinggroup.com

I CAN HELP YOU WITH THAT!

MAIJA-LIISA N. ADAMS

Have you ever wanted to give a TED Talk, but were afraid of being exposed, feeling vulnerable, even feeling naked before your audience? I remember feeling exposed when I was having a Finnish sauna bath naked with a group of women. Do you take a bath with your clothes on? I didn't think so.

Well, we were trapped in boiling heat because two men had parked nearby to survey for a new county bridge for Conant Creek. They were completely unaware of us and I wanted to keep it that way! We needed the cool water that flows from the Grand Tetons. We planned to run, jump and splash in it. Instead, we took a risk that we wouldn't be discovered in order to escape the heat. We silently veered to the opposite side of the sauna and slid in the mountain stream out of their sight without a sound. If you are nervous about standing metaphorically naked before the world giving a TED Talk, I say never let them see you sweat!

I took a risk and 'retired' from my six-figure job as a regional sales manager mid-career to figure out why we weren't successful in starting our family, a family I wanted more than anything! Within three months, I traded the 17 lb portable computer I would lug to corporate, government, education and reseller presentations for a diaper bag! We told God we would take as many children as He would send us, whenever He would send them! We were living in Utah. Our daughter was born two days after Christmas. Two years later we moved back to the Bay Area where our twin sons arrived the day after New Year's and three years later another son was born a few days after Halloween. We were thrilled to have four children in five years! While I was still in the hospital, my husband brought our other children to meet their brother. A stately elderly woman in California observed him walking around the hospital with four children and asked, 'Are they cousins?' He grinned and proclaimed, 'No, they are all mine!'

Aghast she exclaimed, 'You know you can do something about that!' It was interesting to contrast this California perspective with a Utah perspective six months later when we moved back to our neighborhood. A stately gentleman neighbor exclaimed, 'Four is great, but you can do better than that!' After our daughter was born, I was approached about returning to work. When I found out I was expecting twins I knew then it was going to be a while before I worked outside the home again! Luckily, I was able to stay at home with them in California, Utah and in Idaho where we have lived for 17 years. I was a soccer mom, softball mom, dance mom, gymnastics mom, orchestra and choir mom, speech and debate mom, exchange student mom, girls' camp director, classroom volunteer, PTO president and part-time caregiver of my mom.

When a friend asked if I would tutor math students as a paraprofessional at my son's school, I quickly responded, 'I don't remember math!'

A few days into the term, another teacher friend asked, 'What are you doing?'

I questioned, 'What do you mean? I'm tutoring your students!'

She scoffed, 'Yes, for $9.27 an hour. Remember, you are more than this!'

The next year when I heard that a business teacher suddenly left, I told our high school principal, 'I can help you with that!' I took a risk and my reward was a year with my three oldest at the high school. One of the debate kids asked me, 'Mrs. Adams, have you heard of TED Talks?' Little did I know then the reward I had in store from listening to one TEDx Talk, *Start With Why*!

My children and new grandchild are my *why*.

My neighbor who was the communication department head at Brigham Young University Idaho asked me, 'Will you come teach a public speaking class?' My career began teaching information technology at the University of Wisconsin-Eau Claire before I was lured away to Silicon Valley. When I returned to teaching at BYU-Idaho I wanted to teach IT, but staying home and earning a degree in an ever-changing field was a risk I took. Now I wondered if my early choices could bring rewards. What I find common between IT and speaking is the flow of information needs to be well developed to be helpful.

Teaching speech began to reward me even more when I taught a professional presentations class where one assignment was to deliver a TED-style talk. Also around the same time a communication student organized the first TEDxRexburg event as his senior project. The 'x' in TEDx means it is an independently organized local TED event. A local businessman organized the first TEDxIdahoFalls event 30 minutes south. I attended the latter and when the organizer heard I taught public speaking, he asked me if I'd be willing to help coach the speakers. I said, 'Sure, I can help you with that!' At this time, TED granted about 300 TEDx global licenses for events organized around the world. Six years later over 3,200 TEDx events are licensed to be held around the world each year. In 2020 both of these local events were set to be held in March. TEDxIdahoFalls held theirs the first weekend in March and then the TEDx landscape changed with COVID-19. TEDxRexburg held theirs March 2022, two years later! Other events around the world canceled, postponed or met virtually. Since they are independently organized, each event organizer chooses for themself.

My personal TEDx coaching landscape is changing too. My clients come from referrals and entrepreneurs I meet at networking events, mainly on Zoom. Their ideas are varied. Their personalities are varied. Their backgrounds are varied. They want to stand in the middle of that RED DOT that the TED stage has made famous. They want to share their unique perspective of an idea and grow their impact.

My personal path brings the reward of the many opportunities my children and grandchild have. That is priceless! The path to the TEDx stage brings the reward of many opportunities for my clients. I get to see them cross 'give a TEDx Talk' off their bucket list and share an idea that can change another's life. The first person I helped find a TEDx stage was a presenter speaking to a thousand people who mentioned, 'I'd like to give a TED Talk.' At the break I walked up to her and said, 'I can help you with that!' She now has 1.6 million views, a bigger impact and an item taken off her vision board.

If sharing your idea with the world as a TED Talk is on your vision board, I say now is the best time to prepare. Most of us have more time during lockdowns. What would it be worth to you to use your quarantine time to prepare your TED Talk you've always wanted to give? Giving a TED Talk is unlike any other talk. It is not a keynote, it is not three points, it is ONE idea worth spreading. About 90% of TEDx applications are rejected. So, as a TEDx expert, I have seen thousands of applications – and why some of them get picked over others. Have you ever seen someone in your field giving a TEDx Talk and you think, *I should be there?* Maybe you have even applied and been rejected – and you don't know why? Maybe you've heard that you should not use the TEDx stage to grow your business – that it is frowned upon. But then you think, *Well, why do I see so many businesses on the TEDx stage?*

The truth is somewhere in the middle, it's a matter of how you handle the application, that is key – what you say there and how you say it. If you are not sure what your message is, I can help you with that! If you are nervous about standing metaphorically naked before the world sharing your message, I say never let them see you sweat!

MAIJA-LIISA N. ADAMS

Maija-Liisa Speaks
Rexburg, Idaho

Maija-Liisa N. Adams is the founder and CEO of Maija-Liisa Speaks, an Idaho-based TEDx Talk coaching firm. Over the last six years, Adams has helped more than 100 clients understand how to land, nail and use their TEDx Talk to grow their impact and increase their income. As a keynote speaker, she has addressed hundreds of individuals, including the International Women's Day Conference and BYU-Idaho, where she serves as an adjunct professor in public speaking and professional presentations. Adams was a regional sales manager for a $1.4 billion-value global software company. Adams is also an esteemed member of Christopher Kai's GPS global speaker community, where its members include number one bestselling international authors, thought leaders, world-renowned athletes, and seasoned executives who reside in 120 cities, 30 countries and six continents.

Contact: maijaliisa@mlspeaks.com

HAVE FAITH ... ONE THING ALWAYS LEADS TO ANOTHER

DR. DONNA VALLESE

'Just write every word about your business that comes to mind, then play with the word combinations. The name of your business will come to you,' my best friend Jen directed me. We were supporting each other by trading services; I coached her on leadership, and she consulted on rebranding. My son had just left to join the US Navy and now it was time to invest in myself by making my coaching business profitable.

Being a business owner was not something I had imagined when I first started my career in education over 20 years ago. As I gained experience working with children and adults, I began to realize that I was a 'human developer' at the core of my passion and purpose. Every career move I have made has always led to something more purposeful and impactful. Each move has come with risk, but the rewards have always been far greater. Without repeated risk and reward, I would not have evolved into the leader I am today: innovative and transformative.

Within the first five years of my career as a teacher, I led committees, became a mentor, provided professional development, designed curriculum, coached drama club and always had veteran teachers coming to me for ideas. I loved teaching. Today I remain connected to many of my former students and their families. Some of my most memorable quotes from students help describe the kind of teacher I was:

'Whew! I never had to do so many projects in my entire life until you were my teacher!'

'You are the first teacher I have had who truly cares and wants me to do my best.'

'To get drama club back, we should do what the colonists did during the American Revolution.'

'I like to ask you for help because you are one of the few people who will give me honest feedback that helps me know how to improve.'

'Guess what! We figured out how to embed our Scratch animation into our iMovie! Can we show you?'

As a teacher I focused on critical thinking and conceptual learning while ensuring my students knew I believed they could accomplish everything they set their minds to.

Soon I grew to understand that my purpose in this world was much greater teaching one class at a time. I did what many teachers consider unthinkable; I left my tenured position for a series of at-will educational leadership roles. I found job security by being invaluable.

As I embarked on my educational leadership journey, I began to see various styles of leadership. The power of leadership started to become crystal clear to me at the Rhode Island Department of Education where I worked closely with leaders across 53 public school districts and charter schools. I had the balcony view of how well schools with empowering leaders versus ineffective leaders performed. During this time I also joined an activist street band, Extraordinary Rendition Band, which showed me how an organization could effectively function with a true democracy, shared leadership and no designated leader. I observed and experienced how leaders could make or break an organization which became one of the major drivers of my work.

Opportunities began to pop up for me at just the right times. Each role leading to another and each time taking the risk of leaving a place of comfort to continue to grow and make a difference. My leadership skill sets and innovative experiences increased with every role I took. I took advantage of opportunities to experience and lead innovative strategies that most other schools were not doing. As a resident principal, I learned how to turn a school around, and that no matter how bleak a situation looks in a school, with a great leader at the helm, significantly increasing student achievement is possible through blended learning, engaging staff and a community school model. During my time as a founding dean of academics at a public charter school, I deepened my understanding of how to support new teachers in implementing personalized learning with a one-to-one Chromebook program to get student outcomes. Then, as principal of another public charter school for pregnant and parenting teens, I learned how flexible scheduling, year-round schooling, competency-based grading and wraparound supports could completely change the trajectory for students. The case for creating equity for students became another huge driver in my work.

Upon reflection after an unexpected and difficult divorce, I realized living far away from family was impacting me and that everything I had could be found closer to them ... a house, a job, a band, friends, etc. I knew I wanted to work in an urban school district that was on a positive trajectory to make a difference for kids. I applied and was quickly hired by an urban district in central New York. Leaving my life in New England, the support system I had built over 15 years, as well as a job I loved was bittersweet, but it was also another risk I needed to take. This risk afforded me the ability to work with 34 turnaround schools, create impactful development opportunities for instructional leaders, and improve district processes that impacted large numbers of staff members.

During the COVID-19 pandemic, while working from home, I decided to revitalize my coaching business I had started several years prior, but that had gone stagnant as I led an extremely busy life. Rebranding was step one in this new journey I decided to take while still working full-time. This is when I reached out to my best friend Jen from the beginning of my story. Her directive is how Inspiring Leaders LLC came to be.

Because I had already coached and worked with leaders outside of the educational field, I knew that leadership skills were transferable across all professions. I wanted to avoid any possible conflicts of interest with my full-time job working for the urban school district in central New York. So, I decided I would work with leaders of businesses. All I had to do was learn some marketing skills and figure out how to connect to that audience.

My next big risk was to spend the majority of my savings to invest in support to build and market my business. Not only did I learn some basics in marketing and networking, I also learned how to face my case of imposter syndrome. With the support I had invested in, I soon saw that the depth and breadth of my experience would bring significant value to leaders and learned that people will pay for what they value. I started to get excited to talk about my coaching business rather than feeling shy about it. As I gained my confidence over several months, I was still not making money to make up for my investments, so I started second-guessing what I was doing.

But remember, one thing always leads to another. I attended a free workshop offered by Executive Networking Events (ENE) on how to create a free community and a membership. In the middle of the workshop, an epiphany hit me: I am an instructional leader! Why on earth had I abandoned serving educational leaders? Instructional leadership was the one thing I could talk about all day long, every day, and I had put that aside. Why, why, why did I shy away from the one thing that I had worked for over two decades to become an expert in?

In an instant, I decided to squash the gremlin that had used the potential 'conflict of interest' to hide another variation of imposter syndrome. I recognized my need to be serving instructional leaders in my business. Not just any instructional leader, but those who believe that revolutionizing the massive system of education is imperative if we are going to ensure equity for our students while also setting them up for success in our globally connected society.

So, I took another leap of faith and invested in more learning through ENE's Accelerate program. I now have a following of people that is growing steadily every week. I have a platform to speak on about innovative education strategies and a global community of instructional leaders that I strive to support. I lead a membership of incredible instructional leaders who do work that amazes me every day. This membership provides structured opportunities for my people to connect, collaborate, learn and problem-solve together to revolutionize education. I am here because I took risks along the way, reaped the rewards and am proof that one thing always leads to another, just have faith.

DR. DONNA VALLESE
Inspiring Leaders, LLC
Baldwinsville, NY

Dr. Donna Vallese is an instructional leader and the CEO of Inspiring Leaders LLC. Her work in her business and as an urban school district leader is focused on supporting and developing instructional leadership. She considers herself a 'human developer' and has a holistic approach to coaching, supporting and developing the leadership skill sets of others.

Dr. Donna's career in education has afforded her opportunities to work in urban, suburban and rural settings as well as at the district, school, state and university levels. Equity and meeting the learning needs of every student has been a main focus of her entire career. She has had the fortunate opportunity to work with innovative initiatives that make a difference in student learning and outcomes. Her experience has encompassed leading personalized and blended learning, year-round schools, standards-based and competency-based grading, flexible scheduling, online learning and wraparound supports. These experiences have led her to strive towards finding ways to transform and revolutionize education. The depth and breadth of her extensive background brings a unique perspective to coaching leaders with a focus on research-based learning theories, supporting and developing teams, transformation and equity.

Music also plays a large role in Dr. Donna's life as she plays piccolo in a non-profit activist street band that she founded called UNiTY Street Band. Her experience with the arts affords her the ability to easily solve problems innovatively and creatively.

Contact: dr.donnav@inspiringleadersllc.com

DARING TO DREAM

TREZ IBRAHIM

I dare to dream that I can have a different life. At a young age, my parents moved from Egypt to the United States in order to seek freedom from oppression and a life they had dreamt possible. In no place but America can anyone accomplish that dream no matter their race, socioeconomic status, education and religion.

My parents had big dreams. They wanted a big home with a pool and to give their children everything they never had. They wanted to own a farm, live off the land, travel the world and vacation in style. They wanted the freedom to do what they wanted, when they wanted.

I was blessed to have been raised with that same mindset. I could have anything I wanted. My dad always told me to reach for the stars – the worst you can do is land on the moon. I was taught that if I could dream it, I could achieve it.

I spent my entire life believing that anyone could achieve their dreams. So I dreamt. I dreamt a lot. I dreamt of traveling the world, I dreamt of going to Africa to help children, I dreamt of bringing peace, love and healing to the world, I dreamt of meeting the love of my life and living happily ever after. I dreamt of sending my own children to the best schools and giving them the best of everything.

But I wasn't told *how.*

At 21, I got married right out of college and several years later, I had a beautiful baby boy whom I adore. Shortly thereafter was the divorce. I struggled financially for years, was homeless, barely able to put food on the table. I had gained over 85 lbs and was unemployed. I had big dreams, yet my life was a picture of desperation.

My life seemed to get worse no matter how optimistic I remained. The fact is, I always thought having a dream was enough. I believed there was no way I couldn't be happy. Whatever dream you had in your heart would always come true. I had no doubt it would come true.

But for the first time, I began to question that belief. My father slaved over his work for years. Day after day, he wore himself down, saving every penny and trying to invest in a secure and lucrative future.

When I was 16, my father was diagnosed with cancer. He was given two years to live yet died six short months later. He died while he was still working hard and saving every penny.

Ten years later, my mom stopped breathing at a job she hated. By the time she died, she had lost pretty much all of my family's hard-earned money because of poor decision-making.

Neither my mother nor my father lived to see their hard work pay off. Even though I had been broke and struggled, I still went through life knowing that one day my dream would come true. It dawned on me one sleepless night, as I reflected on my parents' big dreams and early deaths: it is actually possible to get to the end of your life without realizing your dream. My parents lived their entire life waiting for their dream life, yet it never came.

This sudden realization put me in a deep state of depression and tore apart everything I had ever believed in, everything I had ever hoped for. For the first time, I was scared I could die without ever realizing the dream in my heart.

One day, at the advice of a friend who knew I had no food for me or my young son, I went to social services to apply for food stamps. As I sat there filling out the application, holding back tears, I kept fighting the voice that asked, *What are you doing here? You are a college graduate, you are smart, you are worthy and you know you don't belong here.* I wasn't ready to hear it, and worse, I didn't know where to go.

Earlier that day, I had scoured through my son's toys and found three quarters; the only money I had access to. I took the 75 c to the gas station and tried to hold in the humiliation as I handed the clerk the quarters and asked for gas. She looked at me puzzled. I held back the tears, looked at the ground and quickly turned around to fill my car up with the dribbles of liquid that would give me a few more miles.

Fortunately, the part of me that grew up believing that dreams do come true pulled me out fairly quickly. That's when I began my search. I began to search for meaning, for purpose, for the secret of how to live the life of your dreams. I studied with a vengeance, realizing I didn't have time to waste. My parents' lives ended early and I learned that life was precious. The time to live, to feel free, to be happy and make every step move in the direction of my dream, was now.

I am happy to say this search opened up a whole new world for me. I learned about taking risks, I discovered the keys to honing in on my vision, I embarked on clearing the path previously riddled with limiting beliefs and decisions. I began to teach these principles, learning even more as I worked with my amazing mentors and clients. And I began to dream once again.

I bought a home, released 85 lbs, dove headfirst into becoming a transformational leader and found love. A man came into my life, swept me off my feet and promised me the world. We were engaged to be married. I opened up a restaurant. It was my dream to create a beautiful place where people would gather and have their senses enticed with an incredible menu and wine list.

It was a huge success. We were written up in papers, had five-star reviews and became a destination spot. I used the principles of manifestation I taught my clients to manifest this dream life. Heading towards opening, with excitement and anticipation, I decided to put my full focus on the restaurant. My five-year plan was to create a successful business that would provide a lucrative stream of income to allow me to work on what I truly loved doing, learning how to *live my dream life* and teaching millions of other people to do the same. I was on track. I let go of my mentors and coaches so I could funnel all my money into the restaurant and released my clients so I could focus on my own manifestation.

This was the beginning of my demise. Sitting in the corner booth of my restaurant, with the lights turned off, I was sobbing. I had to close the restaurant shortly after opening. A series of events had occurred and I was devastated knowing this was the end. I contemplated how wrong I was to let go of my structured system of support, the very thing that allowed me to literally create something beautiful out of thin air. I went on to cry for the next two weeks. Prior to that, the man I thought I would marry ended up being dishonest, lied about who he was and took quite a bit of money from me.

I had risked dreaming and failed once again.

It wasn't long before I picked myself up and began to dream once again. My five-year plan, turned out, was too long for the universe to wait. I was required to step into my passion and purpose now. I regained connection with my mentors and began to share my message. I dove into principles of limitless possibilities, learning to turn those possibilities into probabilities and inevitabilities. Through all my trials, tribulations and opportunities for growth, I have learned resilience, embraced life fully and stepped into a powerful knowing that nothing can ever stop me or anyone who decides to live a beautiful life. Today, I am healthy, vibrant and alive. I live in a beautiful home I absolutely love. I travel the world and do work I love, changing the lives of thousands of people around the world.

And I am still dreaming.

In the words of Rumi, 'When I die, I shall soar with angels, and when I die to the angels, what I shall become you cannot imagine.'

I have big dreams; of finding the true love of my life, traveling the world, impacting millions of lives and working with world leaders to impart a higher level of love and consciousness on the planet. When I achieve those dreams, I cannot imagine what the universe has in store for me. I cannot wait to find out. What I know for sure is that I will always *dare to dream.*

TREZ IBRAHIM
Life Mastery Solution

Trez Ibrahim is the world's leading success master coach, evolutionary strategist and spiritual catalyst working with some of the most prominent business owners, executives and entrepreneurs in the world to empower them to 'live a life by design'.

Trez is the author of four books and has worked with organizations such as Microsoft, University of California, Irvine, Keller Williams Realty and the American Red Cross.

Trained in neuroscience, emotional release techniques, esoteric principles and psychology for success, she has put together the most cutting-edge program for breakthrough results you simply cannot find elsewhere. She shares with her clients a simple, proven system of unlocking the power within you to create anything you desire in life.

She believes that to be truly fulfilled, you need to be living at a ten in every area of your life: having the career that makes you jump out of bed each morning, making the money that supports your desired lifestyle, having the free time to enjoy your life, being in optimal health to get through your day with energy and vitality, and having supportive loving relationships with deep and meaningful connections.

Trez Ibrahim has worked with thousands of clients over the last 30 years leveraging decades of training and a track record of proven results. Trez co-creates with her clients, using manifestation techniques most 'gurus' miss, releasing limiting beliefs and decisions, healing old emotional baggage, releasing internal and external conflict and creating new life-thriving habits.

Within businesses and organizations, she has assisted owners, executives and leadership teams in creating real results, leading high-performing teams and implementing strategies that help them stand out in their industry and reach a level of results far beyond their expectations.

She has worked at the startup, building, scaling and succession stage of businesses. Business owners, with her direction, learn to get out of their own way so they can reap the rewards of their hard work.

Clients continually seek her guidance and support in gaining peace of mind, releasing anxiety and depression, healing relationships and health issues and finding their ultimate purpose in life.

Highly intuitive and insightful, she has been bringing guidance and clarity to clients from all over the world with her keen ability to create a bespoke strategy that creates the quickest, most substantial and long-lasting results. Trez is both dedicated and highly invested in supporting you in creating an exponential leap in your results, at an accelerated rate with extraordinary ease. She is ready to stand beside you and walk with you every step of the way as you create the life you love living.

Contact: trezibrahim@sbcglobal.net

Life Mastery Solution
Your Guide To An Inspired Life

TAKING A RISK IS REWARDING

ANDREW DOBBIN

Over 30 years ago a young man stood in the dock of a high court judge because he had got into trouble with the local police authority. The judge told him, 'If you are with the crows you will be shot at.' Fortunately this young man gained the support of his family, friends and his employer. They took a risk to support him during a turbulent time in his life. It would have been easy to walk away.

Risk has two characteristics, the first being uncertainty and the other loss. Risk is common to every one of us every single day in our lives. From when we wake up in the morning until we go to bed, we make decisions that involve risk. Risk doesn't have to be some big thing, it could be as simple as driving the car or crossing the road. From my viewpoint I don't think I have really taken any big risks in my life, others may believe differently, but I have stepped into risk every single day.

I was privileged to be the territory manager of a large multinational tyre company called ATS Euromaster in Northern Ireland and Scotland. One element of any business is employing staff. You never know if you are going to acquire a dud or a star employee. This is a risk in and of itself, never mind employing a young school leaver with no experience. One 16-year-old called Allister, after a short time, showed himself willing and a hard worker. Were we going to have a winner here?

Allister didn't excel at spelling or writing but he was full of enthusiasm. He was a quick learner and had great hands for the job. Allister got on well with the other employees and was liked by the customers. As a young person willing to learn he was entered into the 'Tyre Fitter of the Year' competition. The management team took him under their wing and coached him through the criteria of the competition. He practised and practised over and over again, honing his skills as went. Not only did he excel but he went on to win the competition. What an achievement for a 16-year-old.

It was a great reward for me personally to see this young man, who was coached and mentored, win this competition. I was so proud of him and of his achievement. This was a reward, but it was soon to be enlarged even more. On one of my visits to his depot, he presented me with a small plaque thanking me for everything I had done for him. I was overwhelmed with his generosity and his gratitude. We could all learn something from this experience.

Both of us have moved on to different careers and businesses in life but we have remained friends and connected over social media. I have watched on as he has developed in life and seen how he has become a loving and providing father to his kids. Sometimes it is just nice to know that you have made a small impact in the life of others.

During the COVID-19 lockdown, I found myself working from home for weeks on end. I had become glued to my seat in front of the computer screen. My only opportunity to get out was to go for a coffee and read a book. Sometimes this was as simple as being in my car sitting outside a local garage. Others found that their way to escape and improve mental wellbeing was to get out and run or ride their bicycle. I was never a great lover of exercise, even though I have completed two marathons earlier in my life. I had a road bike but I didn't ride it enough to call myself a cyclist. One funny moment in life was when I forgot how to get my foot unclipped from the pedal. I fell in front of the parked cars. I'm sure there were a few sniggers that day.

From past experience, I realised that if I was ever to achieve a goal I need to go public and tell others. This is a great way for others to hold you accountable. My fitness levels were on the floor, and I decided to set a goal to ride my bicycle for 200 miles over the incoming month. Before anyone laughs, I realise that this would be a small goal for many cyclists but it was big enough for me, who is a fair-weather cyclist. To help my chances I added a small goal to raise £200 for a local charity. On my first run out I rode for six miles and stopped at the local picnic area where I took a short break and made a video for social media. Very soon I was to receive my first sponsorship money. This goal was very real now. I had to achieve it, there was no turning back.

One of my first sponsorships came from Allister who was to become a supporter over the coming weeks. He not only cheered me on, but he challenged me to raise more money for the charity. Why have you only set a small goal of £200? The sponsorship was to grow with money coming from as far away as India. Allister believed I could do it and he continued to support my challenge financially. The mentee had become the mentor, the roles had been reversed. It seemed so long ago that I took a small risk and employed a 16-year-old. From this small risk, we were to see a young man achieve so much. He not only won a competition which made me well up inside, but used this gain to progress in life. Nothing beats that feeling when you see people believe in themselves and see them achieve more than they thought they could. Now he wanted me to succeed.

It was said of Mordecai that he sought the wealth of his people. The word wealth has the idea of betterment, it is not all about the money. The greatest reward in life is helping others and seeing them succeed. It is about making an impact for good wherever you are or whatever you do. From the time I went self-employed, I followed the example of Mordecai. It became my aim to look to the wealth of others and to add benefit to them.

I have been enabled to do this because others believed in me and took a risk. You see it was me who was before that judge those many years ago. I was at a T-junction in life. It could have gone any way. The important thing was I had parents who loved me, friends who supported me and a boss who spoke up for me. I was only in my first year of employment, but he gave me a wonderful character reference. I continued in my role as a tire fitter for another seven and a half years until my boss was retiring. Just as he was retiring, I was promoted to the role of centre manager where I moved to another depot. He was so pleased with my achievement, and he was rewarded for the risk he took.

Every single day people step into risk which may be large or small. There will be disappointments. There will be the people that let you down and sometimes they don't work out. We need to record the little wins and rewards in life. Write them down and take the pictures. I still have the plaque that Allister gave to me and I look on it from time to time with emotion. There is another plaque that accompanies a medal in my house which acknowledges the first marathon I completed. Some might think that a plaque and a medal is not much of a reward for running a marathon of 26.2 miles. But for me, those plaques mean everything. They represent the rewards on the journey of life.

ANDREW DOBBIN
The Business Mindsets

Andrew Dobbin is originally from Bushmills and now lives in Omagh, Northern Ireland. He moved there originally to look after a tire depot for ATS Euromaster. He is very much a family man—married with three children. Omagh is his base for work and where he is active in the community through his church connections. His work used to be throughout Northern Ireland, ROI and GB. His scope of work has now extended globally due to the shift in society and is now working through online platforms.

His mission is to provide authentic mentoring individually or in a peer-to-peer (mastermind groups) setting where he enables business owners to develop and grow themselves and in turn their business. He is also helping coaches, consultants and trainers create a referral strategy for business growth. His aim is to develop individuals to impact their own life as well as their family and community.

Contact: andrew@thebusinessmindset.co.uk

GOING MAINSTREAM

DR LIZ ISENRING

Why would a seasoned academic, internationally recognized as an expert in their field, in a prestigious, secure and well-paid university position throw it all in to start their own business? Why indeed?! For me, it came down to my values and wanting to make a difference on a grand scale. Join me as I describe how taking the greatest risk of my life has ended in the richest of rewards – better health for others and fulfillment for myself in the process.

I thought I'd be an academic for life. I'm naturally curious and love learning new things. I had reached the heights of my career earlier than most, and thought I'd spend the next few decades teaching the next generation of nutritionists and dietitians, supporting PhD students and discovering the best nutrition to support people through their cancer treatment. However, a few interesting things happened all at once. Sometimes life whispers to you. You can either choose to ignore it or choose to listen and take the risk.

As a busy working mum leading a high-performance team, I was a professor of nutrition and dietetics, head of program and had taken on another role as associate dean of research for the faculty. I was still performing my research at a high level, and I wore several hats including chair of an international organization. I've published hundreds of scientific papers and been awarded millions of dollars in research support (further insights in my LinkedIn profile her-elinkedin.com/in/dr-liz-%F0%9F%8C%8F-isenring-83424065). You may not be surprised to learn then that I was very stressed and heading for burnout. Yet the career highs were still flowing. I was the only Australian co-author on the international nutrition and cancer guidelines that were being highly cited by other researchers and even referred to as the 'gold standard' in the area (gold standard meaning the best we have). It was nice to get the recognition and accolades from this international team effort. Unfortunately, in fairly close succession, I had two friends diagnosed with cancer. Seeing the medical system through their eyes was illuminating and shocking. Both had different types of tumors. Both would say they had excellent hospital care and treatment, yet no-one talked to them about nutrition. One of them described finishing treatment, 'Like being spat out of a complicated system I didn't understand and left to put my health and life back together again.' Why was no-one talking to them about nutrition when we now have strong evidence to show that being well nourished during treatment leads to better quality of life and better outcomes? We'd known about this research for years. Why wasn't it getting to those who needed it? I asked my dedicated medical colleagues (many of whom are chronically stressed and doing the best they can in a less than ideal system). Some centers integrate the different health professions and do better than others but there are certainly huge gaps. How could this be? I soon found out that it takes on average 15 years from nutrition research discovery to becoming part of everyday practice.

People want to be healthy – now! I also don't have the patience to wait that long. I want to help people – NOW. So rather than being a part of the problem, I figured I would be part of the solution. Hence, LINC Nutrition was born.

LINC Nutrition stands for Liz Isenring Nutrition Consulting but also fits nicely with providing a link between hospital and home care. Filling in the gaps with expertise that you would normally only find in a university, hospital or research institute setting. I am happy to say that I live my passion and support people impacted with cancer. However, the more I spoke about my experiences, the more I resonated with busy executives and business owners who could identify with my story. They had success in one or more areas of their life but had not prioritized their own self-care. I now have a nutrition clinic and several online programs. I'm helping people all around the world to improve their nutrition, their health and their lives. I am literally changing lives from the inside out!

'I feel like a new woman, I thought I'd have gut problems for life!' That is what one of my super relieved clients said after her gut problems (diagnosed as irritable bowel syndrome) were relieved after five weeks of working with me. Jan had experienced gut problems for most of her life and these had worsened within the past few years. Her bowel symptoms fluctuated from constipation to diarrhoea with a lot of abdominal bloating and discomfort. Sometimes it was so bad that Jan didn't want to go out to eat in public, so this had really impacted her social life. The doctor and gastroenterologist had ruled out any underlying disease and said that it was most likely irritable bowel syndrome and to get advice on a low FODMAP diet.

Jan says the next year she tried everything from an elimination diet to supplements and seeing a nutritionist and naturopath. While she did experience some relief, Jan says the gut problems were always there and she was fearful of them getting worse. Jan came to see me after her friend, who I'd been helping to manage her unintentional weight loss and fatigue due to pancreatic cancer, recommended me.

We started with a thorough assessment of Jan's medical, dietary and lifestyle history. It soon became apparent that Jan had experienced significant trauma in her life having cared for her ill father for several years and then her husband who had passed away two years ago. Jan was an active member of her community and liked to care for people. In fact, Jan often put the needs of others ahead of her own.

Jan's levels of stress and anxiety were high and she wasn't doing much to help reduce this. We worked on a positive mindset and included simple yet effective breathing and enjoyable activity to help relieve her stress. Jan's mood improved and her gut symptoms lessened. Jan's mindset, physical activity and stress was improving so it was time to tackle what she was eating.

Jan's diet was not providing the nourishment she required. Due to her fear of making her bowel symptoms worse she had a very restrictive diet and was actually consuming a lot of processed foods, even though she believed they were healthy gluten-free choices. By gently increasing her intake of plant-based, wholefoods providing soluble and insoluble fiber, probiotics and naturally sourced antioxidants and phytonutrients, Jan started to feel more energetic and the bowel symptoms continued to improve. By five weeks, Jan was feeling really well with hardly any symptoms. By eight weeks Jan was essentially symptom free. Jan is now training for her first-ever 5 km walk.

'I can't believe I'm doing a 5 km walk!! I would have been worried that I was too far away from a toilet to ever have thought about doing that before.'

This may not seem much of an achievement compared with publishing papers and being invited to speak all around the world, but it was important to Jan. It was important to Jan's family and friends. The ripple effect of helping Jan effectively manage her symptoms meant that she had greater impact with her caring and community work. This ripple effect spreads throughout her community and the world.

What greater impact is there?

While most consider it a huge risk to leave a prestigious, secure and high-paying job, in the end I didn't really feel it was a decision. It was the next step after analyzing the situation. I started recognizing the signs, listening to the whispers that soon became a cacophony. Using my unique skills and education to help others is my purpose. It leads to a deep sense of achievement and satisfaction and gives my life meaning. My message to others is spend time working out and living your values. Once you know your personal values, everything else just falls into place. There are several exercises you can do. It became obvious what was important to me because it was what kept me up at night. Hearing the passion in my voice when discussing the unfair situation to my colleagues and friends made it clear to myself and to others what really mattered to me. Knowing we must and could do better. For years I had created vision and mission statements for my organizations and team, but I'd never done this exercise for myself and my personal values. It was one of the most powerful and life-changing activities I have done. Yes, there are challenges – quite a few, actually – but by reframing these as adventures or part of the journey, and using your values as a guiding compass, helps to lead the way. LINC Nutrition has evolved and it is not the initial business I thought it would be. However, I expand into opportunities as different needs arise. I am having a big impact around the world not just in my research work (which I still continue and ironically my publications are increasing since I've left academia. Is that due to having more time or more motivation? I'm not sure but more energy and better health, certainly!) but in helping everyday people cope with life's challenges and improve their nutrition, health and quality of life. I have teamed up with experienced business and leadership coaches to run 'Being the Change' events, which highlight that to have a healthy business you need to have a healthy business owner. This is taking me across Australia and around the world and putting me in contact with people from all walks of life, including dinner with a billionaire.

While amazing experiences, they highlight that everyone has challenges. Improving health from the inside out is one challenge I can support people with.

I describe myself as a 'recovering academic' who supports professionals and business owners dealing with health scares or stress and burnout to regain control of their life, health and purpose. There is no better feeling in the world to know that you are helping people to live better lives. To see them regain their energy and taking confident, life-changing and proactive steps regarding their health and wellbeing. My research and academic work is having a global impact and helping to improve policies, but I feel most connected to my grassroots work via LINC Nutrition which is helping everyday people, dealing with everyday problems to live extraordinary lives.

DR LIZ ISENRING

LINC Nutrition
Gold Coast, Australia

Dr Liz transforms lives from the inside out! Dr Liz, from LINC Nutrition, is passionate about improving productivity and health via evidence-based nutrition. She has been a professor, head of program and associate dean and is now currently an honorary adjunct professor at Bond University. With over 20 years' experience, she is recognized as an international nutrition and wellness expert and has published over 160 scientific papers and books. Her work is used by over 40 countries and has helped hundreds of thousands of people.

Contact: DrLiz@lincnutrition.com.au

A PURPOSEFUL LIFE

KAREN DESANTIS-MEYER

Let's go back in time to 1995, when I was earning six figures in mortgage banking, the industry was thriving but I wasn't. I was miserable. I was depressed because I wasn't home with my kids. I had a live-in nanny and was constantly nervous about someone else raising my kids and not me. I had no idea how to get out of the corporate America rat-race. I had yet to discover who I was and my true calling. At the time, I didn't know what that was but I knew I was destined to make a difference. I was showing up for other people's dreams and thought I had to fit into a certain mold to get by. That's when I hired someone else to live in my home to take care of my young sons, Daniel and Michael, who were six and four at this time. My energies were definitely not in alignment with my priorities, and something needed to change. I struggled with knowing I wasn't doing what I was called to do, but had no idea what the next journey looked like and where it would lead me. A very sweet friend of mine from high school had moved back from Arizona and shared with me that she had started a new business. 'One of those!' – a relationship marketing business, and I thought she had lost her mind. Why would she do something like that? But, being the good friend that I am, I wanted to support her so I agreed to attend her weekly meeting only so we can grab a bite to eat afterwards and catch up on each other's lives. During the event, I sat in the back of the room, my arms were crossed and putting out, 'DO NOT TALK TO ME. I AM NOT INTERESTED IN YOUR OPPORTUNITY' non-verbal body language. Looking back, I'm sure the director in charge knew exactly how to handle me! But that's when the magic happened. Remember, I was miserable in my current circumstances, not being able to raise my kids, working outside of the house. I started to learn that 'one of those things' relationship marketing opportunity, might be for me. I listened how my friend was going to share her business. I celebrated with a new free car driver that night! She had just earned her first one, a burgundy Pontiac Grand Am. I'll never forget it. She received flowers, cards, and balloons for her accomplishments. I was excited for her. I also learned these folks were earning diamond rings, cash bonuses and lots of support! Little did I realize that I was lacking all of this in my career. No fun, no support, no free cars and no diamonds!

And no excitement in my life. Although, some would say this encounter was an accident, to me it was a 'God Wink' pointing me in the direction to where I am today. I've built a million-dollar empire from home, helped many others build their lifestyles, raised my boys and many more benefits along the way. I never dreamt I wouldn't be in a traditional career, however, corporate America took care of that.

I went against the grain that night, signed my agreement and ran with my hair on fire. Maybe this was my calling? Really, relationship marketing? When I earned my first of six free cars a year later, achieved Queens Court of Sales and top sponsor in my team, I knew I CAN have it all and made the decision to make it my mission to share with other aspiring stay-at-home mommas and anyone who wanted to look and feel better. The most important aspect I learned was that being a stay-at-home mom had been a dream of mine, along with having a career of my own. I didn't know what that looked like until I found myself in carpool lines picking the boys up from school or volunteering in their classes. I became active with the PTA, and I was able to attend all of their filed trips and watch them enjoying their lives alongside them. Homework mom, drying-sad-tears mom, while helping out with the household bills with a second income and a free car. They say that the second largest bill in a household next to the mortgage is the car payment. I would call that a win-win!

Those were some of the best days in my life, being Daniel and Michael's mom. Thirteen years later, the boys headed off to college and my priorities shifted. I was going through lots of changes and my values no longer aligned with that company's. Although my team was thriving, I no longer was and knew it was time for a change. My second round with relationship marketing found me through my love of jewelry. Another high school friend introduced me to her beautiful product line of silver jewelry and I fell in love with it all! So, instead of me being a customer and paying full retail, I decided to jump in again and make a run with it. I loved having the home parties, meeting other people, helping others feel good about themselves. That was a fun three years until 2008 and the recession, no-one was able to indulge in jewelry parties so much anymore. I packed up that business, had a '50% sale closing business party' and then found myself in need of another J.O.B. My definition is Journey of the Broke. Back to clocking in for me and I wasn't looking forward to it. I had to do something, as our household bills were adding up and our income wasn't. My previous husband's business went sour so he decided to retire from it and dabbled in small sales jobs. We were both trying to make ends meet, almost lost our home and barely doing it 'together' as we faced marital challenges. I was finally hired on as a counter manager in the beauty department in a local department store. I worked evenings, weekends and holidays. I was away from the family again, even though the boys were gone, they came home every break and holiday, and my life wasn't with them. One evening while working, cleaning my make-up brushes, the other managers came over to visit near my counter. We were all commiserating how unhappy we were but apparently, I had a smile on my face. One of the gals asked me, 'Karen, why are you smiling? We know you're just as unhappy as we are?' I honestly didn't know why I was but this I knew.

I responded, 'I may be miserable but I know that this silly retail job isn't my end-all. God has a bigger purpose and plan for me.' I had no idea what that plan was, but I knew He did. My faith was getting me through this very dark time in my life.

I held three other corporate jobs from that retail encounter and in 2012, it happened! I was introduced to a night cream that changed the trajectory of my life since. Third's the charm! Really? Another one of those? Another friend, this one from kindergarten, who never did relationship marketing before, offered me to try the night cream and proceeded to tell me I needed to get involved with the business. I was not going to listen, I wasn't interested and I said, 'No, thank you!' I thank her today for being her pleasant persistent self and never giving up on me. She obviously saw something in me I didn't see and said, 'Just try it. Give me your opinion.' I was told I can try the sample bottle for four days. She handed me the bottle and again, like the supportive friend that I am, I did just that. I tried it and LOVED IT. To my surprise, the cream was doing something to my skin within 48 hours. See, I've been involved with beauty and skincare all of my life but I had never experienced such quick results! My sagging skin was firming and my dark discoloration was diminishing. I was pleasantly surprised and told her I wanted to purchase it and become her customer only, not joining the business. She invited me to a wine and cheese get-together to hear more about the product. I figured it was good idea as I had recently relocated and wanted to meet people. We went to a beautiful home in Laguna Niguel, California, where there were about 50 others mingling and hearing more about this wonder cream and the business behind it. Sharp men, women and professionals were involved with this company and something was happening to me. My brain was saying, *No, you don't want to get involved and do one of 'those things' again!* But my heart was saying, *What if?* It's a new company to the marketplace, sharp professionals, men and women. And, wouldn't you know it, I had a business agreement in my hand and I was filling it out. I didn't go to join a business. I went to become a customer. I had no idea why I was joining, however, I knew that if the business wasn't going to work, I had a year of great skin care.

Again, I am who I am. I dove in headfirst and ran! I was coachable and trainable and did everything my business partners told me to do. They said, 'Bottles out, bottles in,' and that's what I did. My friend and I were attending about three to four wine and cheese parties weekly, inviting friends and family to try the cream just like I did. When they started to join my team, I knew we had something special. Within the first two months, I earned the Free Lexus bonus and started helping my team do the same. The following month, I hit the big cash bonus and achieved one of the highest ranks in the career path. I didn't know what was happening but I did know that I crushed through the glass ceiling and wanted to share it with the world.

Travel became a big part of my success. I loved meeting the team all over the world including Colombia, Japan, Australia, Mexico, Canada and South Korea. New York, Texas, Georgia and Colorado were my most common destinations and I met the most incredible people. My team was on fire.

Life was changing and I finally discovered the sleeping giant inside me. My gifts and talents are to help others discover their gifts. You see, a coach once asked me, 'Karen, what is your WHY? What motivates you to get up and do it all over again?'

I answered, 'Honestly, I am happy with one home, a free car, my health and my family's health.'

I finally discovered that what motivates me is helping others achieve what they want. Watching them walking across a stage and picking up their cash bonus earnings and discovering their sleeping giants. I've helped over 100 people earn that Free Lexus bonus and empowered over 40 people to earn a six-figure income and be able to put their priorities in place. That's a win-win!

Finally, in closing, the biggest blessing besides all of the perks, free cars, and of course, helping others, I met my best friend in Neora, my incredibly smart and handsome husband and forever partner Stephen. Our story is a unique one for sure. We started our love affair in January 2015, we were engaged in June 2015 and we married on Thursday 3 December 2015. I will say, 'The third's the charm!'

KAREN DESANTIS-MEYER

Neora
Dallas, Texas

I'm excited about my chapter, 'The Third's the Charm!' for three reasons: my birthday and wedding anniversary land on the third, and I found my final entrepreneurial home in my third relationship marketing company! I hit the jackpot.

You see, I was raised in a traditional business home, attended college, got married, started my family and established a career in corporate America. I really didn't know any different, only that I was serving others and not realizing I was building someone else's dreams other than my own.

My parents raised and taught me to have a strong work ethic as it was a privilege to give to the community, proper values and to always go out and serve others. It's not that I was discouraged to become an entrepreneur, I just wasn't exposed necessarily.

So, after 20 years in corporate America, building my identity and career in mortgage banking and food sales, I started to realize that corporate had no interest in me, my family, my priorities and values. I then discovered that Karen and corporate didn't get along. I was miserable, clocking in and clocking out, not being appreciated with the work I did, and eventually knew that my family was the world to me and I needed to do something about it.

I needed to take my life into my own hands and create a life, not live it for others. I also realized that it's not about 'if' life happens but WHEN it does. I never wanted anyone telling me I couldn't put my family first because of their company's deadlines. I wanted to build a life around my children and have NO-ONE tell me I couldn't.

That's exactly what happened in 2018. When my bonus daddy of over 30 years passed away unexpectedly. Because I had built a home-based business over the last 23 years, I was able to be present with my mom over three months and help her through the grieving process, help her navigate her life – barely going into my virtual office but a few times, and not experiencing a change in my income.

You see, my decision in 1995 to make a shift in my career and my life, to build a business from home where I can raise my two sons, turned into one of the biggest blessings in my life. As long as it didn't compromise who I was, I knew I had my faith and trusted what lay ahead.

Contact: karendesantis@sbcglobal.net

LEAP FROM SOLID GROUND

MINA RAVER

Walking my property, a few tree-dabbed acres in the middle of the Black Hills, is something I could easily take for granted in the chill of a South Dakota spring. The cold makes me bitter, to put it mildly. But the work is necessary. Each of the four buildings on my property have lights, and my three young children get into every one of them in the course of their fairy-ish mischief. It makes me glad I haven't let them talk me into buying horses.

Back at the house now, I hear the boys are still up telling stories. My daughter, the youngest of the three, is sound asleep in the spot on our bed where she knows I will lay when my time comes.

Watching her long eyelashes flutter in the gentle wake of her breath is a treat I look forward to every evening. But tonight, something about this moment, maybe the pink glow of her bubbly baby cheeks, reminds me of a similar night years ago when I stood over my sister's cradle.

Today, as I absorb the warm magic of my child, my shoulders are strong and square with confidence and hard-earned pride. My jaw is set with determination and my eyes flame with clarity. I know who I am and what that means, and that knowledge empowers me to stand firm on the values that guide my life without compromise. That wasn't the case 20 years ago, when I stood over my sister, and I realized that I would have to become her mother.

The walk home from school that night had been frigid too. Fall in Colorado Springs isn't much more pleasant than spring in South Dakota. I could have spared myself the trouble of the cold, more or less, if I'd gone straight home. But I couldn't. I needed to think.

'Your mother called this morning.' It was my first semester in high school, and my guidance counselor and I hadn't warmed up to each other. 'Is there something you need to tell me?'

'No, there isn't,' I growled.

'Can you look me in the eyes and tell me that?'

I let tears stand in my eyes as I turned to bear down into hers. 'There is nothing about my family that you need to know. And whatever that woman told you, she only wants to cause trouble.'

The warthog snorted, 'Is that so? I've only known you a few weeks, but her description of your relationship with authority seems accurate.'

'I have plenty of teachers who would disagree with you. Maybe you just don't know your place.'

'Or maybe you don't know *your* place,' she grunted. Perfect, she was the first to lose her cool. I'd won.

'I know my place isn't foster care.'

'What about your brother and sisters? How many of you are there?'

'We'll be fine. We're always fine. My mother has been coming and going for years. I always make sure we're fine.'

'There are five of you, aren't there? You may be able to take care of yourself, but you can't take care of those little kids. And you father—'

'Stepfather.'

'Right, your stepfather is dying. He needs a high level of care that you can't provide.'

'I've done it so far.'

'How long has it been?'

'Three years. And Mother has done nothing but show up every few months to steal our food stamps. She didn't call you to be helpful. Think about it – if she cared about us, she could just, you know, do the right thing and not leave her five kids. She called you to convince you to take me out of my honors classes. She knows it will hurt me. That's all she wants, to make it harder for me to do the right thing."

'I don't know anything about your relationship with your mother. But I do know that you can't take care of four small children and keep your grades up. I'm going to file a report with the district and suggest all five of you be placed in the care of the state. And yes, you will be removed from the honors program. Now, you can go back to class.'

She smirked triumphantly as she went back to her paperwork. I nodded, grabbed my backpack and walked out. But I didn't turn left into the hallway leading to history. I just kept walking. As my fingertips were chilled by the cold metal of the push bars on the front door, she shouted, 'That's not your classroom!'

'Nope.'

'Look at me!' She'd caught up to me. I turned and looked at her, her flaccid face red and mottled with fury, outright hatred. 'You are doomed to failure if you walk out that door,' she growled.

'If I'm doomed,' I said, 'then it's been that way since the day I was born. But I can make sure my brother and sisters aren't doomed to a life of torture in foster care. And you can't stop me.'

'You know what? I don't care if you leave. You're just a foul-mouth little bitch.'

'Maybe,' I said, turning away. I pushed both doors with all my might and let them swing open as if thrown by a storm. 'But I'm not your bitch, and that's all that matters.'

I was 13 years old, an angry cauldron of fearlessness and bravado. I felt ready to take control of my life and future, even if it meant leaving the clear path of high school to college that I'd always dreamed of. But the adrenaline wore off with each step. After a few blocks, the fog cleared from my mind, and I had nothing to do but think. Really, deeply think.

Besides my family, school was the only thing that mattered to me. My mother hated me, my stepdad resented me – but at school I shined. My teachers loved me. They went out of their way to give me tough problems to solve, answer my questions and preserve my curiosity.

If I was going to give my brother and sisters the opportunity they deserved – the opportunity our parents couldn't provide – I'd have to give up everything.

Could I really quit school? Was I willing to give it up? If not education, then what did I value? I had to think about it. I wandered the streets of Colorado Springs for hours, trying to imagine who I would be without school – without my gifted classes, ROTC, band and my Knowledge Bowl team.

Who would I be? Doomed?

I couldn't do it. I had to run away. So, I went home to pack.

Back at the apartment, everyone was asleep. The dinner dishes were still laying out on the table. Dad and my little brother had fallen asleep watching *SpongeBob SquarePants* on the living room couch. My sisters were asleep in their separate beds in the room they shared. The baby, my youngest sister, slept in her crib in my room – lights off, door closed. Her hair was matted to her face and it was clear she'd cried herself to sleep.

I dumped out my schoolbooks on the edge of my bed and sat down to think about what a runaway would need on the road. My thoughts were shattered by my sister's sudden shudder. It was cold, and she wore nothing but a diaper.

As I laid her blanket over her, I wondered who would keep her warm when I left. How many nights would she cry herself to sleep in a cold, dark, empty room? Who would she grow up to be on her own?

Who would she be if I left her? Doomed.

And I would be too, doomed to a life of compromise and weak, shifting values. I'd have nothing to hold onto but the fear that drove me away.

I lifted my sister from her crib and lay with her in my bed. That night, I made a promise to myself. I promised I would have it all. I would find a way. I promised to have faith in infinite possibility and the gifts I'd been given to let my values guide me.

I've thought of this moment a few times, the moment I became the woman I am today. I thought of it when I became the first in my family to earn a college degree. I thought of it when I started my business, when I decided to launch my campaign for Congress. And I hope that, someday, I think of it again when my children ask me to tell them the secret to living a meaningful life. Because that is the day I will know, beyond the shadow of a doubt, that I have served my promise well.

If you want to break glass ceilings, you've got to leap from solid ground. Our values form our footing. If your footing is weak, if your values are constantly shifting beneath the weight of your options or what seems available to you, you'll never stand on solid ground. You'll never get a good leap. You'll never reach the ceiling, much less break through.

Don't compromise. Plant your feet on firm values and refuse to settle for anything less than your whole vision. The risk is great, the reward immeasurable.

MINA RAVER

Forging Fortune
South Dakota

Mina Raver is a super-achiever out to prove that whatever you hope to gain from life, compromise won't get you there. Especially when it comes to your values.

Mina is the eldest of five children, from a family with a history of poverty. Low-income and often homeless, things took a turn for the worse when her mother chose to abandon the family. The decision came after her stepfather's diagnosis with terminal illness, three weeks after her youngest sister was born.

Faced with an impossible choice, Mina defined her values and has leaned into them ever since. She dropped out of school in ninth grade to raise her four siblings on her own but never gave up on her dreams. She realized her dream of becoming the first in her family to earn a college degree by turning the world into her classroom. That dream came true in 2015, just four months before the birth of her second child.

Since graduation, Mina has had her scientific research published internationally, become a successful entrepreneur, been a Congressional candidate, an internationally acclaimed speaker and a published author. And, at just 35 years old, she's just getting started!

As the founder and director of Forging Fortune, Mina teaches purpose-driven entrepreneurs how to turn their passion for change into a powerful justice business. With her signature program, entrepreneurs and small business owners all over the world are learning to achieve unlimited influence, affluence and impact – the true meaning of prosperity.

Mina lives in South Dakota with her husband Mike, their three children, three dogs and one ornery cat. The family lives by an important motto: Every good thing in our lives is evidence of our responsibility to others.

Contact: waraver@gmail.com

CANCER CURED MY MINDSET
(REWIRING THE FIRE FOR PASSION, PURPOSE AND DESIRE IN A LIFE I LOVE)

DAWN GADEN

All eyes on me. I'm standing on this stage. Over 100 people are waiting to be inspired, motivated, educated by me. How did I get here? This is a dream! Am I really here? I have to pinch myself. Does life really get this good? This is really fun!

My life has had a lot of funny moments. At the least, raising four boys with my husband, Mike, reveals the great comedies of living! Having two boys, two miscarriages, followed by identical twin boys. Now that's a roller-coaster of fun-filled, upside-down, topsy-turvy belly laughing, cry-'til-it-hurts moments.

This, right here, on a stage, standing confidently in my own skin, that's a whole new level of fun! Many would shrivel up to a glob of sweaty goo on the floor before speaking in front of an audience.

Sure, I have some jitters, get a little flush, but I am so excited to be here now. My true purpose, my true passion in life is to inspire others to live a life they love, to thrive and live in abundance, and experience pure joy!

So how did I get here? Sure, I bought a ticket, flew from Michigan to Ireland – who hasn't? Staying in a castle, launching a book, surrounded by professional, authentic, inspiring humans that lift and support each other. You've been there, right? Okay, maybe that's a bit more rare. But why? Why not risk it all for the dream of living big? My husband would often say to me, 'If you want it, you always make it happen!' I think that is one of the things that I love about myself – I go big, take the risk and make my life how I want it to be.

This was not always true. I spent many years wearing that superhero cape that stifled my wings. I was so busy rescuing everyone else, I got left behind.

It took some shifting, changing and risk-taking to get to where I am now. This was a path full of obstacles turned opportunities. This was the adventure of a lifetime, and so much more living to come!

Here is one of the many (and possibly last) superhero stories in the life of Dawn, that I would like to share with you now. Remember, we're all human, so sometimes old ways sneak back in. The trick: be aware of it, embrace it with love and take another path. We are 100% responsible for our lives. Maybe not what happens to us, what comes along in this world, but how we respond, that's on us. Here's what happened when I needed to really shift my image and choose another way.

I'm living the dream – happily married, raising our four boys (twins included!) in our dream home in the woods. I was able to be with my kids to raise them and work part-time after completing my master's degree, inspiring others through change and growth.

I spent many sunny days with my boys playing in the backyard, running through the sprinkler on hot summer days. Belly down in the grass searching for bugs and eyes in the sky shapeshifting clouds into animals. Catching frogs and fireflies and taking in the fresh air and blessings all around us. Stargazing before bedtime and storytelling by moonlight.

And then it all changed. This life got turned upside down once my husband lost his job. My beautiful life was swept away within an instant. Within months we went from two children to four, a new home in the woods and no job! Now what?! We have four children to feed, a mortgage to pay, bills – the fear set in.

Time to take care of business. I was really good at coming to the rescue and fixing the problem. So here I go again, I put on my superhero cape and off I went to save the day. My old self-image would take hold – I tie on my superhero cape and come to the rescue. Be aware, no-one asked me to, this was my old story, my old self-image, how I defined myself. And here I am, no more beautiful sunny days in the backyard picking flowers, or daily hikes in the woods. I am now surrounded by windowless brick walls, cameras in every corner, metal doors slamming shut with the press of a button from a faceless figure behind a one-way glass. Working in the county jail seemed to be the right fit, and would take care of the unemployment issue. Unfortunately there was little desire for an inspired life, roadblocks to bring real change to so many who needed it (and some who truly wanted it).

I'm fueling myself with coffee and self-loathing. I am resentful, depressed, angry and feeling a sense of unworthiness. Brick after brick, no longer able to serve or inspire others, I begin to build a prison around myself of depression, sadness and hopelessness.

I sunk deeper and deeper into depression, I felt worthless. No longer serving at work, and completely drained to be of any light or joy to my husband and children. The prison I created for myself of unworthiness, self-doubt, shame and resentment – that prison is what kept me from living my life.

Disconnected from my dream, living on autopilot, sleepwalking through my life.

I knew it was time to wake up when I wanted to escape my life. On that dark rainy morning, another tearful commute to work, I heard a fearful voice. 'Just keep driving, it's no use to go back. You are worthless, no benefit to anyone, you don't even have the energy to be a good mom anymore. Mike can handle it, he can figure it out.' But then a small, still voice whispered, 'It's time to wake up.' You know that voice? I know you know that voice. That voice that we often ignore. That voice of love, kindness and compassion.

I chose to listen to that voice and ask for guidance: God, you have to give me something else; this I cannot handle.

Shortly after, during the prison of self-doubt, shame and blame, I was diagnosed with cancer.

You can imagine my conversation with God after that: Are you kidding me! Really, cancer? I can handle cancer?!

Well, I guess that was up to me.

I decided that cancer was my escape – my opportunity to live my life again. I had a decision to make, a shift in my mindset and image – *who do I choose to be now?* Coming to the rescue and saving everyone else left me depleted, depressed and destroyed. I had to choose who I wanted to be, take off the superhero cape and spread my wings.

After a heart-to-heart with my husband, we had big decisions to make – career, cancer, healing practices, parenting. I left my job, Mike was still unemployed at this time – a huge risk! We were living on faith and passion to live our best life. This was the first time since I was 16 years old that I didn't work! I took time off to be with my kids, to heal my body, mind and spirit. It was time for a shift, to create my life as I choose. We took family trips again, played in the backyard, hiked and simply enjoyed each other.

As I healed and began to fall in love with my life again, I started my own practice, Mind Body Counseling & Coaching. I was re-energized to follow my passion and pursue my mission to serve others and create change in the world. I traveled to NYC and became a verified intenSati leader. Teaching this mindful practice is the core of all my work. I am now an international speaker blessed to have shared my message with audiences from the Bob Proctor Coaching Program (one of the world's leaders in personal development). I have brought my mindset expertise to world-class programs such as Speaking From Within Speaker Spa Retreats. I am a leading voice in my field of The Image Shift – creating a powerful positive self-image so that you can live a life you love, a life of love and a life worth living!

I am deeply blessed and grateful for my family. My boys have now outgrown me, two in college and two in high school. Mike and I love every minute we have with them. We travel and explore the beaches from California to Florida. We live life as an adventure worth savoring. We get this one go-around and we are going to shine!

Creating conscious living is my personal life mission and one I want to teach others. No more sleepwalking through life. I invite you to take off the superhero cape, spread your wings and fly!

DAWN GADEN

The Image Shift Coaching
Michigan

Dawn Gaden is the CEO of Mind Body Counseling & Coaching, a licensed counselor, international speaker, author and successful entrepreneur.

Dawn is a powerhouse in the field of personal development. She is internationally known for igniting positive change.

Her global coaching program – The Image Shift, 3 Secrets to Manifesting the Life of Your Dreams, is powerfully transforming professional women's lives around the world.

Dawn has devoted her life to studying with the best in the field of change work. Dawn has been mentored by speaking icons like Bob Proctor and Wayne Dyer, and has spoken on stages and podcasts to over 10,000 people.

Dawn has over 21 years of experience as a licensed counselor, coach, registered yoga teacher, and has a unique expertise in changing the brain with exercise and activating your energy in a practice called intenSati.

As an intenSati leader, Dawn teaches her clients a whole-body experience that creates lasting sustainable change and powerful image shifts that forever impacts their lives.

Dawn was born and raised in Michigan where she currently

lives with her husband Mike of 22 years. She is raising four amazing boys that includes 16-year-old twins! She especially loves paddleboarding, taking long walks on the beach and going on wild adventures across the country with her family each year.

But she is most grateful for the gifts she has discovered through her journey with cancer. It was in this experience that Dawn learned to thrive by living from a heart-centered place, choosing to never compromise her joy and happiness for struggle and limitations.

Contact: dawn@createconsciousliving.com

THE LONG WAY AROUND

DEANNA BATTE

I stood frozen with tears running down my face watching the water, that was gushing from a broken pipe in the wall, cover the beautiful white tile that graced the floor of what was left of my 'dream business'.

The last of the furnishings were in danger of perishing. My gorgeous amply curved walnut desk, the fountain with stones from the only opal mine in Idaho, beautifully lit shelving where my handmade/custom precious stone and sterling silver jewelry was displayed, stained-glass window-hangings, spiritual artwork, beautiful hanging lights and wall sconces, scrolled ornate full-length mirrors … I drifted into my head, picturing in detail how beautiful it all was.

My dreams, my money, my reputation were being packed into the back of a big moving truck. And the water kept flowing … there was no way to shut it off. The weld had broken in the copper piping inside the wall.

The water main was locked in the lava-rock-walled basement

of the building next door to the beautiful 75-year-old building, and both our landlord and the next-door landlord were unavailable. The only other way to shut off the water was the shut-off valve on the outside of the building – underneath the manhole in the middle of the street, directly in alignment with the front door.

It was after-hours at the city water department. I called the emergency number and after the longest 45 minutes ever, there was a city water employee climbing down into the street where the manhole cover had been. The water was still running from the wall.

The ten minutes that passed seemed like forever when he resurfaced shaking his head saying he was going to need a large compressor to move the shut-off valve … it had corroded in the open position from many, many years of no motion. As I watched him hop back into his truck and drive away, I wondered if this was a final cleansing of the energy after the storm of deception had finally moved on.

My thoughts and feelings went to a place six years earlier. This space was a flurry of excitement and planning. Walls and ceiling were torn out, a new furnace and plumbing installed, new lights, electrical, beautiful and unique light fixtures, creamy large stone-like tile, wood laminate flooring, beautiful glass, tile archway, a spacious office and clean packaging room for herbs and remedies, were all created.

On the other side was a lovely fountain that sounded like you were listening to a quiet stream. There were all the beautiful furnishings of a well-appointed upscale salon with full-length mirrors, perfect lighting and a plush yet relaxing reception area on the other side. Feng shui was rampant and I was giddy with excitement!

In part because I had dressed in coveralls and boots for the demolition and clean-up, partially that I had also done much of the construction and painting. I had invested literally everything into this new venture. My 16-year marriage had ended three years prior, my health had turned around from a dismal state to a healthy and energetic state, and I had gambled all of my money – not a small sum – into the renovation and seed money to begin a new life, creating the business I'd always wanted: to help women heal on the inside and realize their outer beauty as well.

I partnered with a woman who loved the office end of business and was very accomplished at it – or so her credentials said. Being most productive and happy as a creative, it seemed perfect to let my partner do what she loved. We both trained in intense courses from the guru of salon and spa management as well as leadership. We were on the same page as far as business was concerned (or so I thought). We opened the doors to a new and very different business in our region: yoga, meditation, personally designed wellness and weight-loss programs, astrology, card reading, reiki and other related certifications, and an upscale salon with very experienced and talented professionals. Essential oil and energy medicine were available for natural support of emotions and physical imbalances.

It was perfect. Business was good.

Until it wasn't.

We were growing quickly in a business whose concept was new to our area. Being very public about energetic healing was a gutsy move.

It seems that I have always been on the forefront of new ideas that become more mainstream years after I open 'concepts' into the public sphere. That's another story …

For five years the doors were open. Revenue was climbing and clients were happy and referring us to their friends. Life and business were good.

Then things shifted. Red flags turned into red flashing lights!

Suddenly my purchasing power was limited. Other odd things were happening and I was denied access to the accounting.

Red flashing light!

Only later did I find out that credit cards were being opened in my name and bills weren't being paid. My money and good credit rating were gone. I was more than $50,000 in debt. It's hard to describe the emotional state I was in with words. Shocked, ashamed, disappointed and defeated come to mind.

I was fortunate. I still had me (barely), and I had a very supportive network of people who constructed a net of safety so that my fall wasn't fatal.

I was able to find a house that was structured perfectly for my business. There were separate floors and entryways. With a bit of renovation, it was transformed into a beautiful, safe space.

I secured funding with the help of a close friend and moved my business into the ground floor. The upper level was my beautiful sacred space and for a while very few people entered.

My clients were so supportive and kind, and I began again.

That's when the real work started. My own work to understand why I attracted partners – personal and in business – whose agendas were to clip my wings and control my money. This time there was nothing left! I admit, I allowed it. There was a pattern here. I had to explore it and answer the questions that were running in my head, mostly at night when I was supposed to be sleeping.

I found a mentor, someone who would call me out, and honestly not many people could see me deeply enough and had the courage to do that! She did call me out and taught me much about myself.

My intuitive abilities that I had shut down as a young girl were awakened, and my energy medicine client list grew.

Then I found another coach/mentor and continued my climb up the ladder of self-discovery. Of course, it wasn't a steady climb, sometimes I needed rest or I tripped, but I got back up and I grew. As I grew, I shared. As I shared, more growth came and as that new growth was revealed, everything shifted, me included. Business and personal relationships grew along with my business revenue and my confidence. I was growing exponentially in every area!

My client load was increasing so much that my waiting list was six weeks out. In the personal service business when you are scheduling that far out, that's the signal to raise prices.

So I did – a lot.

As a rule, you can expect a 30% decrease in clients when you close a business, or move, or raise prices. This didn't happen at all! In fact, my list was growing!

Working so closely with women in a private setting, I knew their stories and guarded their secrets. As I worked, I was given answers to guide them … not always, but many times. I was also able to connect them with others who would benefit them. The answers just came into my awareness, sometimes in words, sometimes as pictures.

I was becoming known as the 'it' stylist and color expert who would give intuitive sessions with your color service. As much as I loved doing just that, I knew that I was giving myself away. A total business mistake and it was exhausting! I learned and implemented appropriate boundaries around when the flow of intuition was allowed to come in and when it wasn't.

Don't worry, I'm not reading you right now!

That's when I was guided to train as a certified intuitive strategist. Yes, that's really a thing. It's important to have structure. Then a certification in EFT (emotional freedom technique or tapping) as a wealth coach.

Combining my life experience, training and knowledge of business, I set out to even the scale for women. Did you know that 80% of women begin their careers with the disadvantage of a lower pay scale and conditioning that unless they are uniquely qualified for a job, they need not apply?

My personal strength and understanding skyrocketed as much as my client list and I now have a very successful coaching business serving businesswomen in the international market. My retirement funding is recouped and my credit restored!

My journey to living a prosperous, joy-filled life has not happened without its challenges, yet the growth that comes through is priceless.

DEANNA BATTE

The Feminine Phoenix
Idaho Falls, Idaho

Deanna Batte is an expert mentor helping women have clarity around the unconscious patterns that sabotage their success. She is a powerful deep listener – detecting the solutions and connecting women to their own vital personal resources. She instills confidence and empowers transformation with tools that improve health, money and relationships.

Deanna is an international speaker, thought leader and gifted healer who has helped thousands of women grow confidently and take inspired action to overcome personal, family and business challenges.

Deanna has trained as an intuitive strategist, life coach, reiki master and EFT coach. She has worked with women on a deep and personal level for over 30 years in her business and volunteer programs. She has a deep personal understanding of the pitfalls and conditioning that women experience in their lives, rising above her own circumstances to become the standard bearer for women and their affluence.

Contact: deannalyn57@gmail.com

 The Feminine Phoenix

A REBEL SKIING IN VIRGIN SNOW

THOM DENNIS

I can't say that all my risks have paid off, but each decision I have made has led to life taking a new turn, and either opening or closing a door, but always with learning.

One of my early reflections of this was when I managed to join the UK high board diving squad at Crystal Palace. Now, I was never that good a diver, but just being there with those people opened up many opportunities for me. It highlighted a sense of daring and adventure that years later saw me diving off very high cliffs in Malta – one of my outstanding memories.

When I left school, I did not go to university, choosing rather to go to flying college, but I was actually thrown out halfway through for 'scaring' my instructors! I took a job in a factory just so I could make good money to be able to keep flying. My main aim was to fly solo, and honestly, the first time you do is truly a golden moment. I can still remember it clearly to this day.

I continued working at the factory, flying when I could, and it wasn't long before the company offered to put me on a track to be a manager with a clear aim of becoming a director of the business. That was at a time when most people stayed working for one company for their entire lives, and being given the opportunity to work your way up to the boardroom was a dream. But the rebel in me had other ideas! To everyone's surprise, and particularly my mother's chagrin, I decided to discard the secure potential, both in terms of finance and status, and join the Royal Marines.

What if I had stayed in the factory? Working in the same place for years – just for the security. What experiences would I have missed out on? I'm sure I disappointed many people with that decision, but I won't forget my boss, the production manager who really honored my wish to explore!

The Marines was a great time of learning and more risk-taking. I remember one time in particular when I risked my reputation by following my instincts. While in Malta, I had a marine in my troop who was a big burly guy who was always in trouble, and we didn't know what to do with him. He would get drunk and into fights, constantly a rebel, but I had a sense about him. Maybe the rebel in me recognized the rebel in him. I went to my company commander and told him I wanted to promote the man to lance corporal. After a bit of persuasion, he shook his head and said, 'Be it on your own head.' But following my instinct really paid off that time. It turned out that after I had told the marine, he went straight to the clothing store and bought himself a complete set of new kit. The next morning on parade he was immaculate – beautifully pressed trousers, shirt, and of course, the new single stripe on his arm. And from that day on he wasn't in trouble anymore. He really responded to being given responsibility in the most positive way.

And I think I've done that quite a lot over the years, I see something in someone and take the risk. I am not afraid of taking them on and encouraging them to give their best. I've had some bumpy moments along the way, but that's okay.

When I left the Marines in 1991, I don't think I was particularly realistic about my skill set. I was very confident and wrote around 200 letters to different companies offering my services. When I didn't receive a single reply, I decided I would have to start up my own business – Captain Thom, coaching business leaders. The name arose from the popularity of Bowie's song 'Major Tom', and the fact that I'd just left the Marines as a captain. I trained as a business coach with the only coaching organization in the UK at the time, but really the training was more about how to use the *Yellow Pages* and a phone! In those days, one could often sweet-talk a PA and get through to the CEO. I would say, 'You don't know me, but you need me. When can I come and talk to you?' It really was a numbers game – sometimes it worked and many times it didn't.

My next business partnership was a 'big risk'. I joined up with the head of the coaching arm of the consultancy where I had trained. We had big dreams. He wanted to take books and tapes to the mass market, while I wanted to get into coaching leaders in large organizations. We got into the big banks in the city and were running advanced, T-group style personal development courses. We took our clients on a fantastic journey and achieved great results, but with every high often comes a resultant low, and some of our clients would 'crash and burn'. We weren't offering follow-up support and there has to be a safety net when people go through those sorts of experiences. My business partner was pretty explosive and very gifted, but I found the way we were running our workshops to be irresponsible, so this led to my first adventure into therapy, learning how to deal with his personality and mentally protect myself.

In 1994, I embarked on a master's in change agent skills and strategies. Because I had taught at postgraduate level at the Royal Naval College in Greenwich, I was able to go straight in without completing a bachelor's first, but I found it tested my confidence a great deal. The ethos of the course was very humanistic while my training in the Royal Marines had made me excessively sure of things, and this made my fellow students very uncomfortable and reactive to me. I came away more humble and certain of far less.

In the same year, I set up my next business, Phoenix Obsidian. The name had very powerful meaning for me. The phoenix is a beautiful bird, mythological, of course, but its story is that it lives for 500 years, dies and then is reborn, rising from the ashes. The point for me was more about its longevity than the rebirth. The invitation to my clients was to ride on my back to gain a bird's-eye view of their whole life's journey. Obsidian is volcanic glass used in healing and is very grounding. So the core message was: fly with me, but we'll stay grounded. I had some wonderful images created for the website – which is still live, by the way, though not very active – and I loved how it put over my message.

In 2009, my marriage broke down as I experienced a very strong pull to the US. In retrospect, it was a huge risk, but I followed my heart, left the UK and moved to Houston where my main client was based. What I really wanted was to be out in Wilderness Park. I was looking for a way to immerse myself in nature.

The CFO of my main client, a multinational organization contacted me and said, 'Look, we really like how you work with us, and we want to do more, but can you do something a bit different?' I had already discovered the work of Bert Hellinger and family constellations and had seen a demonstration of working with horses in that context in Holland. So I sought out a therapist and horsewoman locally. They were having amazing results healing people, particularly with trauma and drug problems. We created some corporate programs that blew everyone's minds: horses are ultra sensitive and feel what is going on in humans, even at a sub-conscious level – you can't lie to a horse! Any bullshit that might be going on within a team is mercilessly revealed!

That adventure turned into six extraordinary years where I ended up marrying the horsewoman, exploring Wilderness, and living on a ranch in the mountains outside Denver. We ended up with a herd of 14 horses and worked with individuals and large corporates. That remarkable phase of my life kind of blew up very much how it had started, but it was a great example of how taking a risk can reap rewards.

After my return to the UK, I took the risk of starting up (another) business. Serenity in Leadership was created in the wake of realizations I made while on retreat in Guatemala. I had seen how CEOs can often reach the pinnacle of their careers and yet still have a kind of void which leaves them dissatisfied. This causes them to go searching, for instance on ayahuasca retreats or attending Burning Man, but to me, it's the tension between the dysfunctional masculine and the largely suppressed feminine that is calling for resolution. How can we be leaders while being at peace and keeping our hearts open?

I've had a number of moments in life when I have been able to say I was very peaceful. One was with the horses – if you're not at peace ... they don't like it! Another was during some of the retreats I've attended, for instance with Jill Purce, practising

Mongolian Overtone Chanting. When you chant, your inner voice is quietened.

When you know you are at peace with yourself, you can experience higher levels of serenity and happiness. I'm very clear these days that happiness comes from within. When we search for it outside of ourselves, we are seeking ways, or other people to make us happy, but life doesn't really work like that. It's important to realise that while our connection to the universe is absolute, the volume of our inner guidance is soft. With all our internal noise going on, it can be difficult to hear.

And that is, I think, the great power of meditation although I do not in any way claim to be an expert. I find it difficult. I've never been diagnosed, but I think I might have ADHD, as concentration is either total or it's non-existent for me.

Part of the practice of life is to enjoy it and appreciate it as you go. 'Life is,' as Dan Millman says, 'a series of moments.' Looking back, I can see that every risk I have taken has led me to where I am now. It's all part of the journey and the story of my life, and the reward is in the living of it. Each risk has gifted me amazing, although not always comfortable, experiences. Like the time I went rafting down the Grand Canyon, oblivious to how risky it was until I was there.

Taking risks may not always have immediate rewards, and certainly may not play out as you expect, but ultimately will lead to a more passionate and fulfilling journey. In living my life, I have been less conscious of risk at the time of decision, and more knowing that what I was choosing to do was right. It was only on reflection afterwards that the level of risk I had taken became evident.

As Mary Oliver says in her poem about the explorer Magellan:

Let us find our islands
To die in, far from home, from anywhere
Familiar. Let us risk the wildest places,
Lest we go down in comfort, and despair.

THOM DENNIS

Serenity in Leadership
West Bergholt, UK

Polymath and social entrepreneur, Thom has run Serenity in Leadership, the premiere leadership development and culture change consultancy, for 30 years. He is passionate about bringing awareness to those in positions of power and leadership, so they understand themselves more deeply and care profoundly about the impact they have on their people and the environment their organizations touch, both directly and indirectly.

His journey has taken him through many careers: engineer, pilot, Royal Marines officer, coach, healer, facilitator to agent of change and keynote speaker. Each experience has colored his sense of what good leadership looks like in varying circumstances and how traumatizing the abuse of power is, whether driven consciously or otherwise.

Thom's personal development and awareness journey has led him to an ever-growing understanding of the parts that ego, trauma and feeling play in our behavioral make-up and he is now focused on helping the feminine take her full place in society and business, both in men and women. His aim is to enable the feminine to shine and to bring equipoise to the dominant masculine, whose negative energy and traits pervade so many of our institutions, and whose positive aspects are so lacking. He sees this approach as a pivotal route to fostering real inclusion and thus eliminating harassment, bullying and the abuse of power in all its forms.

He has been featured on both BBC TV News and radio and as a thought leader in over 100 articles in industry leading publications in just 2021 alone.

He is well-known for his expertise in creating transformational change and is a sought-after advisor on a spectrum of leadership, diversity, inclusion and justice issues.

With over 30 years' experience as an executive coach, facilitator, change-maker and leadership developer, Thom has helped bring about responsible leadership and enabled change in corporations in the US, South America, Europe, Africa, India and the Far East. He has been hired by global banking, pharmaceutical, energy and engineering brands such as Citigroup, Royal Bank of Scotland, Pfizer, AstraZeneca, Conoco Phillips, Shell, BP and ABB Automation, to name just a few.

He holds an MSc in change agent skills and strategies, is a certified facilitator accredited by the CQ Center, a certified NLP master practitioner, a member of the International Association of Facilitators and a Fellow of The Royal Society for Arts, Manufactures and Commerce.

Thom served 17 years as an officer in the Royal Marines, has lived and worked in many countries, and is the proud father of two and grandfather of five. His extensive travels for both work and pleasure have informed his understanding of different cultures, and he is working on a second book. When relaxing, he can be found delving into his library or combining his love for nature and wild places with his curiosity in photography.

Contact: thom@serenityinleadership.com

FROM $9 AN HOUR TO $900,000 GROSS

JENNIFER YORGESEN

I had been a stay-at-home mom for many years. Raising four kids didn't come without its challenges, but we managed the best we could; it was tight. My husband, Brian, is the master at budgeting and was affectionately called 'Brian the Budget Man'. We had what we needed, without a lot of extras, and that worked well for us. It wasn't until my youngest started school that I decided it was time to get a job to help with the finances.

I got a job at my local school working as a secretary, and I absolutely loved it. I loved being around the kids, I loved taking attendance and meeting with the parents; the social aspect and the fast-paced environment was where I thrived – not without incredible hard work, of course. I was making $9 an hour.

Within the same office, there was the secretary – me – who got minimum wage, and then there was the contract secretary. They made about $14 an hour, they got health benefits and an official contract. So, when the resident contract secretary left a year into my employment there, of course I applied for the job. I was confident in my skills, I had been working incredibly hard in the past year, and quite frankly, I was pretty good at it.

The principal gave the job to somebody else. This was someone who came from a completely different department of the school, so when they started they had no idea of the processes and functions of how things worked in my department; I ended up being the one to train them.

After about a year, that same person moved on to a brand-new school that had just been built. I applied again for the contract secretary position, and once again, they gave it to somebody else. Someone that also didn't come from my department; I would have to swallow my pride a second time, and train them as well.

I'd been there for two years by this point. I was well liked, I put in extra hours, was never late – I deserved that darn job. So, I picked myself up, marched over to the principal's office, sat myself down and said, 'Hey, I've done this job for two years and helped to train the last secretary in the very job I applied for, and was more than qualified to have been given it. Could you please tell me what I've done wrong?'

His response: 'You didn't train them, the district trained them. And hey, at least you've got a job.'

It's safe to say I quit that job.

I was feeling pretty worthless after that. There were many tears that came after realizing how unqualified I was; I didn't have a degree, I hadn't worked since college and I wasn't sure what else I could do that was beneficial and would fit in with my schedule while still having the time to care for four children.

Finally, after months of searching and a whole lot of personal growth, I got my real estate license. I passed the test – a big shock to me, and frankly a big 'woo-hoo' moment. Unfortunately, I quickly found out that the test hadn't really prepared me for the career ahead of me. The test was just facts and figures, it certainly didn't teach you how to run a business, do taxes, payroll, marketing, how to find business for yourself or what to do if you found any business – all it taught you were the laws.

I had no idea what I was doing. That's where the learning came in. It was, and still is, incredibly difficult to get into this business and be successful. It's something like three out of every five agents don't make it past three years in this industry – most quit. I was determined not to be one of those people.

I started small. I went to a bunch of classes and started networking and listening to members of the industry who could give me some insight into how to succeed. Most importantly, I worked hard. Incredibly hard. I can outwork anyone, except my husband – he's a workhorse.

Eventually I started getting clients, I started building and negotiating contracts and knowledge in the industry. And I was pretty good at it. I realized that I do actually have some skills. This was closely followed by the realization I was now responsible for my clients' biggest purchase of their lives and all the legal details that go with it. This was accompanied by a lot of sleepless nights. It wasn't long before the imposter syndrome slowly reared it's ugly head.

This is a fluke, this is just luck, there is no way this is going to work out. The fear was real, I still believed I wasn't even good enough to make $9 an hour.

And my imposter syndrome was visible. Three years and several awards into my career, my wonderful neighbour approached me with a very enlightening question: 'Jennifer, why are you still driving your old Prius?' My Prius, which had been the vessel in which I shoved countless items to show and stage houses through the years. My tiny little Prius. My Prius that had been paid off, for years, and yet I was still holding on to, just in case I didn't succeed.

About 4.5 years into real estate, I found myself crying and stressing a lot – not because I was failing, but because I had no time anymore. I was making plenty of money, I had more clients than I could handle, and was winning multiple awards, and I was way too busy. It was unsustainable.

So, I started researching and educating myself on how to run my business. My mind was totally blown by the 80:20 priciple, that 20% of the work creates 80% of the benefits – and therefore you should be delegating the other 80% of the work.

When I left Coldwell Banker that year, in search of a way to learn more, to think bigger, better and more efficiently, my broker told me I shouldn't leave. She said you will just be a small fish in a big pond at Keller Williams. I thought, *Well, then, that is exactly why I need to leave. I can't grow in a small pond!*

I was so nervous at the new place. Those top agents were hitting numbers I had never imagined possible and I felt inadequate. However, I jumped right in, stretched myself, let myself be vulnerable to grow. Since the move to the big pond, I have tripled my business in 2020 and was the number one solo agent at KW Westfield! I went from crying, trying to keep up with 44 transactions, to closing 86 transactions in 2021 and even had some free time. (FYI the average real estate agent closes less than 12 a year.) I started learning passive income streams and have been able to invest in a title company, a home and auto insurance company, a lending company and in a land development project. Then we personally purchased not one, but six, rental properties in three years! Two of those are nightly rentals in St George, Utah, close to Zion National Park. We didn't have a clue what we were doing when we started but just kept moving forward. I now have an administrator who helps in the business, an amazing husband who supports and helps on the backside and I have been able to bring my son, Cameron, into the business full-time too. Last year, as a brand-new small team we were the third top performing team in our brokerage. So much for being a small fish in a big pond!

Not getting that job and being told no was the best thing that ever happened to me. I have learned so much, grown so much and have met so many amazing people who have helped me along the journey. Besides my career of helping others create wealth through real estate, I also get to teach, attend top producer functions and rub shoulders with those creating businesses and those who give back in a big way. Not only do we now have enough money to pay the bills, I no longer have to drive that little old, run-down Prius and Brian the Budget Man can have a break. Instead of stressing about the budget he helps me build! And the best part is it has given me more of an ability and means to serve and help others. The skills that I have learned in real estate have also taught me to create events and bring the community together and the means allows me to run with it! For example, what started out as a client event three years ago has turned into the 'Best Christmas Ever' for six families! This is not only Christmas but a major life-changing gift. In three years we raised over $50,000 in donations to help six families by not only providing Christmas but we have paid medical bills, paid lots of rent, purchased a car, helped with construction projects in homes, sent a family to Disneyland whose dad had cancer and sent a sweet family to a family reunion in Hawaii after the loss of their dad. Each year it grows bigger and bigger with community support and I have made lifelong friends.

Can you even imagine if I had got that promotion at the school? I am pretty sure I would still be there taking attendance. Sometimes the best answer is no. A no just means you need to go push a door open. I can't wait to see what other doors I can bust open. This is just the beginning!

JENNIFER YORGESEN

YOR-View Real Estate Team at KW Westfield
Orem, Utah, USA

In 2014, Jennifer Yorgesen left her $9 an hour job at a school to pursue a real estate career, with hopes to earn $10,000 to make ends meet. Last year alone, Jenn, now rainmaker and founder of YOR-View Real Estate team, completed 86 transactions and personally did 76 of those. She well surpassed her goal of $10,000 within the first month of 2021. Although her résumé boasts of these great top producer achievements, multiple investment properties, assertive, strategic manoeuvres in her career and people who now rely on her for their income, what people know her for is her loving and caring personality. Not only does her family – husband, four children, their three spouses and three and a half grandchildren – love spending time with her during Sunday dinners, family vacations or just hanging out in the hot tub and watching movies, but she is also often found selflessly serving others in the community. Being a real estate agent has given her the opportunity to sponsor 'Best Christmas Ever', which is near and dear to her heart. She may be one of the best at home design, negotiating, marketing and being organized when it comes to real estate, but the reason her clients keep referring and returning to her over and over again, is her care beyond the transaction. She prides herself in knowing every single one of her clients have been served and received the best treatment and deal possible in their purchase or sale.

They may start out as clients, but they end up friends. Her motto is that there is always someone you can learn from and there is always someone who can learn from you. She's an example to all, both new and seasoned on what it means to be a great real estate agent and friend.

Contact: jennifer@yorview.com

CHOOSE YOURSELF

DALLAS KING

The weight of my black wool suit is nothing to that of the occasion I find myself in. The flagstone floor beneath me has worn to a high-gloss polish under the passage of hundreds of years' worth of people on their way to and from the verdant green of the gardens, to the comforting embrace of the castle itself. The stiletto heels of my Louboutins, with their vibrant red soles, are solid underneath me, a foundation of my very own. Even though I am in a room of glass and metal walls, all I can currently see are the nine minutes ahead of me. Luckily, the windows in the conservatory don't reflect all the things I've felt before taking my place in front of a room of my colleagues.

The people in the room with me are silent, sitting in orderly rows of foldable thrones, each a CEO or owner of a business waiting for me to begin. Looking out at them doesn't bring the nervousness that generally accompanies a speech. More than anything I feel a kinship with them. They are a roomful of powerful and amazing people, and I have worked hard to be here with them. Together we are a band of believers, friends in a common cause.

We are entrepreneurs who have all built and helped each other.

And we are family ... This is the reward I promised myself two years ago.

Not the shoes, the Louis Vuitton bag I brought with me or the custom-made suit.

Not the room in the castle that feels like home. Or even the trip halfway around the world to meet them.

The reward is the knowledge that I belong. That I am just as worthy of my success as any of these giants I call friends.

That is my reward ...

Only four years ago, my world was vastly different from my reality now.

I was lost in a hell partially of my own making. I had no identity outside of my roles as wife, mother, friend, daughter, sister and co-worker. I saw my value only if I was useful or helpful. A person to be acted on, instead of someone to act. I tried to find satisfaction in losing myself to those expectations. I left job after job to be with my children as they grew, only to fall into a pit of depression and launch into another job where I could feel useful in another way.

Neither situation filled me. I was giving my all, and rarely was I replenished by it.

In an attempt to find myself and my power, I joined one direct sales company after another, as many women are wont to do when desperate to find some autonomy. I swore to myself when I joined the fourth that this one would be the one that 'stuck'. That I would be one of the wildly successful ladies I saw in the Facebook groups with their free trips and shiny cars. The only problem with that plan was the desperation I brought with me: the lack of feeling worthy.

During the chase for success, I was introduced to someone

who would ultimately become my mentor and help me unlock the prison gates of limiting beliefs. Together we worked on the lies spinning around in my head, my fears, and most importantly, my dreams. I learned how to find my own answers and work toward my ultimate joy.

A month after we finished our course together, I was determined to know which way to go. I had been empowered with the ability to ask and receive the answer, so it remained only to figure out what my calling was. I had always known that there was an exceptionally specific thing I was born to do, I just had absolutely no clue what on earth that was.

So, with a determination borne of a desire to stop having reason to question everything, I armed myself with all the things I could possibly need to lend me the strength and guidance I wanted, and retreated to the only quiet place in the house – my bedroom.

I spread my journal, scriptures, notes and phone – complete with a mediation playing on a streaming service – and prepared myself to receive my answer.

The experience that followed was the most real, most tangible, most solid feeling I'd had the opportunity to experience up until that point; but it was also the most ethereal, most out there, most unreal high. I was filled. Every cell, every particle, was full of knowledge and its truth bowled me over spiritually. While I was being fed, I also felt a detached sense of doubt.

This can't be real, can it? What if it's all just in my head? What if I'm just making it all up in an effort to feel something?

Almost immediately, the answer came. There was no way it wasn't real. The knowledge was literally burning through me, how could I deny that? How could I not accept what was clearly a certainty?

Before the experience had closed, I had spent an hour on my knees beside my bed, writing in my journal all the thoughts, feelings and impressions I had received in that time. I knew without the slightest hesitation that I had received my answer and I could finally see a way forward. I knew where I was headed and what it was that I was called to do.

From that day forward, I have been walking that path, physically and mentally. Every decision I make I base on whether this will help me go further on my path. I saw the opportunity to sign up for a networking group to help make connections and have the backing and support of other wildly successful business owners. I had no way to pay for it, I wasn't making money yet, but I risked it.

I asked for guidance from one of my new friends, a person who pushes me in so many ways – but always for my best – and received some advice that led me to step outside of my comfort zone and start a YouTube channel. I had no idea what went into a channel being successful, or even what I would talk about, but I risked it.

I met another individual who has taught me so much about marketing and how to position myself as an expert on my own journey and what it will look like for others. Again, I knew nothing about how to present a confidence I had only just found and am still learning how to acknowledge in a real and genuine way, but I risked it.

And here I stand, slightly shaky and unsteady in my most expensive pair of shoes, reaping the reward of the work I have put in so far. Knowing that this abundance is all because I said yes while my mind couldn't see any way forward. This is my reward …

Looking back on it all now, the risks of not starting on this journey were far greater than I realized at the time.

Had I not recognized my unhappiness was a result of my choices, or lack thereof, I would have continued to bounce from one thing to another. I would still be trying to find fulfillment in actions or jobs that didn't use my potential to its fullest. I would most likely still be behind a desk and suffering, wondering why I dreaded going to work every morning when it's a good-paying job that takes care of my family's needs.

I could have gone back to just being home with my kids. And it really would have been 'just'. I didn't wake up every morning happy and abundant because I got to be home with my sons. I woke up grateful that at least I didn't have to go to work in a place that was okay, but also slightly toxic, only because it wasn't what I was meant for.

The risk of not waking up would most definitely be me still believing that I was only meant to be someone who was useful for something. I would have based my self-worth on whether or not I was out helping all the people around me. I would have seen life not only as a mountain of tasks to complete and projects to start, lose interest in and then abandon, but also as one long drudge from one person's needs to another's without ever seeing any relief for my own.

The risk of not working on myself and my limiting beliefs was that I would miss out on the fullness of joy that I now feel is my daily norm. I wouldn't have the direction or purpose I have now. I wouldn't be able to wake each morning with the knowledge that my worth is inherent, and not based solely on how much I am putting out for others.

The reward is the knowledge that I belong where I am standing. That I was right about me.

DALLAS KING

Dallas King Coaching & RJK Acquisitions
Utah, USA

As wife and mom to two teenagers, Dallas divides her time between her family, her work with women as an empowerment coach, exploring new shops, reading books and trying to do yoga without pulling anything.

She and her husband own a taxidermy brokerage that specializes in buying and selling high-end trophies to discerning collectors.

Dallas' coaching and Facebook group aims to help women who are burned out in their daily lives and traditional roles to find joy by rediscovering themselves and their power and authority.

Dallas grew up in the heart of the Rocky Mountains of Utah, until a family move when she was 17 took them to Star Valley, WY. Ever the city girl, the urge to get back to Utah was so powerful that in 2015 she and her husband Bob, and their two boys moved.

Contact: dallasleann@hotmail.com

DEFINING MOMENTS THAT LEAD TO PERSONAL FREEDOM

KEELY WOOLLEY

I can safely say, I finally love myself.

This might seem arrogant or self-absorbed, but believe me, it has changed my approach to life and has benefited everyone. It took me 50 years to realize the 'people-pleaser' mindset isn't a positive trait.

Ultimately it lead to my burnout and without realizing, behaviors that were less than pleasing to others around me. Ironically creating precisely the opposite of what I was trying to achieve. I have finally begun to love myself and in doing so, I have become a better person. The people-pleaser has gone, I can say 'no' when I want to. Life isn't a constant competition or a race, it's a journey of discovery, bringing with it new experiences and challenges to be embraced and not feared!

I can proudly say, that since May 2020, I have become the founder and managing director of KW Consulting Services Ltd, helping mid-size businesses to global corporate companies to 'stop flogging a dead horse' and being stuck in endless debates about what is right for their business to 'deliver excellence'. I have since created Metamorforsuccess Inspiring Leadership Endeavour, a coaching and training program, to help business owners, leaders and entrepreneurs find their why, and turn it into reality.

Ironically, this achievement was as a result of a significant change in my career. Previously, I had worked within a global packaging and paper manufacturing, FTSE 100 company, as group procurement director – head of program delivery. Responsible for driving the development and delivery of the procurement corporate plan, strategy and complex high-value strategic programs and projects, with my team of project managers. Which is where my journey begins.

In November 2019, I am sat in this large white conference room and there she is, sat across from me, with her usual quiet self-assured gentle manner, watching and listening to me struggle to find the right words as I break the bad news to her. 'All of us will be put at risk for redundancy whilst you are on your honeymoon. It's horrendous timing, I know, but I have to tell you before you go, I want you to hear it from me and not through the grapevine.' I was devastated, telling her we were more than a team, we were like family, the biggest difference is that we all picked each other.

Saying sorry just didn't seem enough, but instead of her showing disappointment, anger or frustration, she showed maturity, professionalism and said, 'Keely, you can't take care of or be responsible for everyone, we are all adults and we are old enough to take care of ourselves. Your priority is taking care of yourself.' This nugget of wisdom was shared by my youngest team member Laurine. A piece of advice I should have listened to.

But regardless of those words, each time I had to repeat the message to another team member, I felt responsible, and I was dying inside. All the time, my focus was still on them, their future, and not concentrating on my own or truly preparing for the roles I was being interviewed for.

In December 2019, I am surrounded by people all rushing to airport security in Schiphol, and the noise around me is overwhelming as I place my passport on the scanner, and I can feel my breathing gradually become more rapid. My heart is racing and I just keep repeating the car crash of an interview in my head over and over. As I make my way up the escalator, my legs buckle at the top of the stairs and I collapse to the floor sobbing and sobbing, oblivious to anyone walking past me. Eventually a security lady asked if I needed help, but by then I couldn't breathe or talk coherently. I'd had a complete meltdown and panic attack and had to be taken to first aid in a wheelchair, put on a monitor and given medication to relax. There was no way they would let me on my flight until they could find some semblance of normality. What more of a wake-up call did I need that I wasn't looking after myself? Yet I still kept concentrating on others, making sure they had secure futures, and not once considering myself.

Inevitably the call came; after investing 23 years of my career with the company, my boss told me that I had been unsuccessful with the interviews and was now at risk for redundancy. This hit me hard! From that moment, I physically and mentally shut down, I could no longer function and inevitably signed off sick. I hadn't been listening to the previous warning signs and my body just decided enough was enough. The super resilient me couldn't socialize, I couldn't find the right words or speak properly, the panic attacks and the crying continued, just stepping out of the door was inconceivable.

During the first month I typically recycled every conversation and situation leading up to their final decision. As you can imagine, all my self-belief and self-confidence in what I know I did well I started to question and began doubting my capabilities, no matter how many people told me otherwise. Then in March, whilst talking to my therapist, he asked if I knew what imposter syndrome was and continued to say, 'It is when you are subconsciously lacking self-belief and constantly seeking approval. Which means that you keep trying to prove yourself to others and want to prove you have earned your seat at the table along with your other colleagues, particularly the male ones.' Of course, I immediately recognized this behavior when I was at work. I'd always said yes to everything, volunteered myself to yet another task or challenge, rather than say no. Work was all consuming, I had no room for my own personal life and without realizing it, I had become a stressed ticking time bomb, just waiting to go off. I had no time for myself personally, and subsequently, wasn't fully present with family, friends or colleagues. I was just spinning plates and waiting for them to collapse around me.

It was then that I first realized I needed to make some changes, but before that I needed to focus on the here and now. I still wasn't ready to spend time talking with family and friends, but I began to walk my dogs every day, a luxury for me, as previously I was travelling constantly. This helped with my healing process, my anxiety attacks became less frequent and I started to truly notice my surroundings, become more mindful of the here and now, instead of rushing from one location to another. I actually found time to time to listen to the sounds around me; I began to notice the birds singing and the bees buzzing. The noise in my head had stopped.

I started to enjoy gardening, I actually achieved more in one year than I had in 20 years. I never realized it could be so relaxing, I'd previously seen gardening as a necessary chore. Who would have thought growing your own flowers, from a seed, would be so satisfying and give you such a sense of pride and pleasure?

Gradually, I started to socialize with my close family and friends, but one day at a time. By then, COVID-19 had finally become a reality for everyone and lockdown ensued. Ironically this resulted in helping with my healing process. One hundred miles away, a close friend's daughter had to transfer all yoga classes to online and I decided to give it a try. The yoga classes were just what I needed, it taught me to focus on the present, relax and meditate, concentrate on my physical and mental wellbeing, and more importantly, to stop repeating the past over and over in my head.

Should you or someone else in your life ever find yourself in a similar situation to mine, experiencing that meltdown, these are the three steps that helped me on my journey to recovery:

1. Taking daily walks in the fresh air, noticing my surroundings and being mindful of the here and now, yet still allowing myself time to process the situation, without pressure to be in company and only talk when ready.

2. Being at one with nature, enjoying the garden, growing and nurturing plants and flowers, finding a distraction.

3. A physical and mental activity, such as yoga for relaxation, mindfulness and meditation, and focusing on the present.

Now here was the dilemma, I still had to make some life-changing decisions about my future.

Particularly with my contract finishing at the end of April 2020. However, the more I spent time at home with my family, the more I came to realize that work wouldn't define who I was, but how I behaved would and there can be a balance, and it was important that I found it. So, how could I ensure I didn't get sucked back into the same cycle of behavior, competing essentially against myself, and always pushing to achieve more, trying to prove to myself that I was good enough?

There could only be one option and it didn't include the rat-race of a corporate world in a full-time role. So, on the 15th of April, my 50th birthday, I decided to take a leap of faith and made the decision to set up my own consultancy business. I wasn't naive and knew there were risks associated with this.

Especially the financial risk, particularly with my husband being medically retired and no other regular income into the family home. I knew it would mean personal commitment and hard work, particularly in the beginning. I knew there was uncertainty and things I had to learn, lots of unknowns, even *known* unknowns.

Despite the obvious risks, I could only see the benefits and opportunities that this path would bring personally. Crucially, my own time and destiny was my responsibility and no longer determined by a corporation. I would be free to be real and authentic, and not behave in a way that I thought was expected by others, a 'corporate persona'. The success of my company would be determined by the values, beliefs and ethics, that I represented, 'my brand would be me'. I could work with clients who shared a similar mindset or choose to step away if they don't. It would allow me to work with like-minded people, who are passionate about what they believe in, and why they exist.

So, why am I sharing this, you may ask? To show you that we are all human, any of us, no matter how strong we and others,think we are. We all have a tipping point, and the outcome can be catastrophic. For some it can be irreversible, they relive the past and reflect those thoughts into the future, resulting in depression, self-loathing, anxiety etc. and we need to be mindful the impact these events can have on people and how we respond to them.

I consider myself very fortunate. Gradually, I did bounce back, and came out of it relatively unscathed, but definitely changed. It gave me space to reset, reflect and reshape my future, thinking about where I went wrong, but most importantly, it helped me to think about what I did well. I am proud of what I have achieved, where I have come from and where I am now. I am successful, successful in life, I have a beautiful family and amazing friends.

Since setting up KW Consulting Services Ltd in May 2020, I have successfully achieved a turnover 50% higher than my than my highest full-time income. My first client has extended my contract three times, because of the visible results I have helped them to deliver. Through Metamorforsuccess Inspiring Leadership Endeavour coaching and training program, I have helped my clients to not only find their why, but make it reality. Furthermore, I have overcome my fear of marketing and sales, become an international professional speaker, recorded video blogs and run webinars. All of which has been achieved during one of the most challenging periods globally with COVID-19. The greatest benefit of my business has been working from home full-time and spending time with family and friends.

KEELY WOOLLEY

KW Consulting Services Ltd
Utah, USA

For me there is nothing better, than seeing the shine in someone's eyes, when that light-bulb moment occurs and they discover their 'why'. Then being a part of their journey to help make it reality.

I'm a coach, mentor, change agent, business strategist and program delivery executive who decided take a leap of faith and step away from the corporate world so that I could help to inspire others to be even more successful and fulfilled in life and business.

I'm a proud mum and wife of 30 years, living on a little island called Sheppey in the UK, where we share our home with two slightly bonkers but extremely cuddly German shepherds and a very cute fluffy independent cat.

Physical health has always been important to me and I love being outdoors, either cycling, walking or camping. Although, more recently, yoga and meditation has become an almost daily routine, which has helped improve my physical and mental health.

I have a passion for travelling to new destinations and meeting new and incredible people, whilst discovering and tasting different types of food and drink. I am also a great lover of live music, particularly watching and listening to musicians play Django Reinhardt gypsy jazz, 1940's Hot Club and jazz swing. So much so, that I have travelled to the International Django Reinhardt Festival, in Samois sur Seine, France, for over 20 years.

If you would like to learn more about me and my company visit: www.kwconsultingservices.co.uk

Contact: keely.woolley@kwconsultingservices.co.uk

Metamorforsuccess

I GOT FIRED, SO I HIRED MYSELF

LORA CERULLI

I just got fired. Oh my God. I just got fired.

My phone still by my ear, tears pouring down my face, I hear my now ex-boss saying, 'Lora ... Lora ... Are you still there?' I hear him then grumble to himself, 'I knew she would be difficult.' Me – difficult in this situation? Boy, that is hardly how I would describe myself right now. I then hear him say, 'I am passing you to HR.'

I am a proud finance graduate from one of Canada's top business universities, Concordia. Known to be a pure extravert, analyzing future and present values of financial products was not going to be my thing. So, I decided to sell financial products. I had a passion to explain, represent and sell mutual fund investment products. I thought it was ultimately the best investment product ever created. No matter if you have a lot or a little, if you are a risk taker or risk avert, one can find a mutual fund perfectly designed for your needs and investment profile.

Driven by this passion, I climbed the corporate ladder. At the age of 30 I was promoted to the dream job in financial sales, regional sales representative and attained my career and financial goal. I was mandated to travel within two Canadian provinces, presenting my line of venture capital funds to thousands of financial advisors. I would warmly pitch and present how well our funds diversified into any investment portfolio. Our funds invested in IT and scientific startups and I was privileged to bring along scientists, doctors and engineers with me on the road and have them present their inventions.

It was an exciting role, and it paid the six figures I always strived to reach.

This role was taken away from me in April 2007. I was devastated. Tears kept streaming down my face. How was I going to tell my husband? We were newly married, just had a baby and bought our first home. Sheer panic.

I now hear the HR lady over the phone. 'Lora, you there? Oh, Lora, we are so sorry. You see, we are going through a corporate restructure and ...' *And you are getting rid of me, passing my responsibilities to my inside sales rep at half my salary. Got it.*

Ouch.

She proceeded to put a bandaid on my wound with a modest severance package and ushered me off the phone.

I was insulted. Sad. Hurt. ANGRY. Worried. Then ANGRY again! Looking at my new baby girl now about nine months old, I just wept and worried.

No more extra cash to buy her fun baby clothes. No more splurging. We had to now live on a tight budget. Ah, damn, I hated that. I studied and worked so hard, devoted years of service to this industry and to now be living this catastrophe.

We were now dependent on my husband's salary, which thankfully was a very good salary that fortunately allowed us to pay our mortgage on our new home and put food on the table. But, we needed a second income. What in the world was I going to do next? I had never ventured outside of the financial industry.

I took this dismissal so personally because I took this role to my employer as my personal mission and obligation. An obligation to excel at my job and reach every sales target they threw at me. I was a proud employee.

How easily I was thrown out for their financial convenience. No remorse. No 'thank you' nor 'I am sorry'.

My depression was getting worse.

I had to snap out of it. I had a baby to care for and a household to run. I began to ponder on what was the real reason for my frustration. What was really and truly causing the disturbance to my inner peace? We all know that the truth of the matter is that we cannot blame anyone for how we feel. It is true. It is so easy to point that finger and blame someone or something for your hurt, and keep on hurting.

My state was not their fault. This was just an occurrence in my life. A situation. Yes, a great inconvenience, but the reality is that it was a blessing.

As the old saying goes, one door closes and another opens. It is a GIFT when a door closes, you see. Even a BIGGER gift when the door slams into your face and hurts you! Many don't realize that this is an ultra-exciting experience and blessing. There are gifts that really can overflow into your life from such harsh situations. The slammed door naturally presents and offers many new doors to be opened. And the ultimate gift is the liberation to choose the door you fancy to open and explore what is behind it! It is exciting.

At the time, in continuous panic, I looked at my husband one evening and asked him, 'Mike, now what? Seriously, Mike, what will I do?' His reply was quick, natural, so matter-of-fact and full of confidence. He replied, 'Now, Lora, you will be a recruiter.'

I looked at him like he was crazy and mocking me. I never studied in HR. I never had to hire or fire anyone! I was the one hired and fired. Before I said another word, he continued to explain, 'You see, Lora, you love people. You love helping them out and you are such a sincere and active listener. You love to connect people. I see you do it all the time. You also have a business acumen. You can help companies find the right new hire.'

I hate to admit it, but he was right.

Still too depressed to get out of bed, Mike submitted my résumé to a local recruitment agency. They called me for an interview and hired me on the spot. I was still badly bruised from my experience, and I admit, this new job paid less than half my salary I was fired from. Yes. That ego can be a loud beast. You must shut it and tame it down so you can think rationally and logically and listen to the sweet cheerleading sound of your heart.

I stuck to it, and I LOVED IT. Forget the small salary, I just adored what I did all day long. My soul sang! When I made my first placement and found a perfect candidate for my client, I was in tears. That ability to directly help a human being find not only a great job, but the right working environment just made my heart sing. I was actually directly responsible for finding a great new employee that was happy to work in the environment I proposed. This resulted in a happy team, a harmonious work environment and continued prosperity for the employer! I was in heaven. I found my art.

In the meantime, certain industry practices did not sit well with me and went against my core values.

I therefore began to dream of creating my very own recruitment service company that would allow me to provide an authentic service to employers, not only understanding the criteria of the role they are trying to fulfil but their work environment, culture and values. In capturing the essence of an employer, I wanted to hunt down candidates in line with the employer's values and mission, thus significantly reducing the expensive risk of a bad hire and help foster a prosperous employer-employee relationship.

Explaining this to my husband, he encouraged me. He told me, 'Lora, quit. Tomorrow go register your company calling it, Personnel Chez-Vous. The word "personnel" is a play on the word, cause you find personnel and you are so personable. The "Chez-Vous" in French, meaning "your place" works well living here in Québec, and heck, it's cute! Lastly, hand me all your credit and debit cards.'

It was a gamble. A risk. This time I was quitting and leaving behind a salary and back on a tight household budget.

I worked hard. It was scary but it felt right. I hustled. I networked. I was on a MISSION. I started to connect people. I started to earn an income.

Fourteen years later, Personnel Chez-Vous is an incorporated company that has serviced thousands of employers in Canada and the US.

The reward of taking a risk of running your own business from ground up, is the sheer proudness and gratitude I feel each time I am given a new mandate by my clients. Their trust is my reward each and every time. It keeps me going. I am authentically grateful.

Do what your heart desires. Put some brainpower and logic into it, sprinkle it with love, care and TONS of patience, as you would to a newborn baby. A little prayer for luck doesn't hurt and then just experience the reward of attaining what your heart desires and what you deserve.

LORA CERULLI

Personnel Chez Vous Group Inc.
Montreal

Mother. Wife. Entrepreneur. Forever growing.

Lora Cerulli was born in Montréal, where she completed her studies. She completed her DEC at Collège Jean-de-Brébeuf and then majored in finance and international business, receiving her Bachelor of Commerce from Concordia University in 1996.

She is a daughter of immigrant parents who came from Campobasso, Italy, in the 1950s.

She entered the world of finance as an assistant to five financial brokers and worked her way up to a position in client services for a major Québec-based mutual fund company. Within 18 months she was promoted to regional sales for South-Western Ontario. From her new office in Toronto, she offered business development solutions to over 1,000 financial advisors in her territory.

In 2000 she was called upon Mackenzie Financial Corporation and offered the position of regional sales manager back in her hometown. In 2004 she accepted the offer as a regional wholesaler for Eastern Ontario and Québec, to promote GrowthWorks capital, a Vancouver-based venture capital firm, to all Eastern Ontario and Québec financial advisors.

Corporate restructuring took place while she was on a

maternity leave for her firstborn. This resulted in an abolished career she worked so hard to achieve. Such a circumstance, albeit devastating for her, provided an opportunity for her to truly explore her real passion. Her husband, recognizing her natural skill at connecting people, encouraged her to explore the world of recruitment and headhunting.

In 2006 she was asked by a large, national recruitment agency to start up their accounting and finance permanent placement recruitment division. Unsatisfied with most industry practices, she launched a company that, until this day, reflects her values of dedication, passion and professionalism.

In 2008, while on maternity leave with her second born, Lora founded Personnel Chez-Vous, a recruitment company that embodies both spirit and skill. She launched a business where she could do what she loved, her way.

Today the company is incorporated under the name PCV Group Inc. and helped thousands of people find not only the right job but also the work environment that corresponds best to their values and ethics.

For anyone having met her, the words positive energy, knowledge and ambition probably spring to mind. The contrary would be difficult to argue.

Her moto: no resting until the job is done. She takes on a mandate to match the perfect employee with the perfect employer and she's fully committed to getting the job done.

What she still loves 14 years later? Connecting people.

Today she still resides in Montréal, Canada. She lives with her supportive and loving husband and her two children. She strives to build long-lasting memories and takes the family to Italy every chance she gets. In her free time, she indulges in the art of bread making and cooking for her family and has a passion to continuously learn from her mistakes both in the kitchen as well as in business.

Contact: lora@personnelchezvous.ca

DIRT DR. TO PHD IN FOLLOW UP

ROBERT H. ROSENTHAL

We were living in Centerville, on Cape Cod in Massachusetts.

I was managing a motor hotel after moving from New Jersey. I loved the business of dealing with people on an intimate basis.

Very service oriented.

The situation was, as was in New Jersey, and probably still is … the weather … cold, rain, hail and lack of warm weather.

We finally decided to move to California with all its positives in reference to weather.

Yes, there were and still are earthquakes and forest fires, but so be it.

So, I gave notice, rented a U-Haul, hitched the car and headed to my parents in New Jersey to drop off my ten-year-old son.

My wife and I drove to Atlanta and took a right turn for California. We had a time element because we needed to arrive before my son's plane arrived. We were successful. We drove the 3,000 miles without ever backing up because I did not know how to pull a car behind the U-Haul.

Once, I had to help a lady change her car tire because she was stuck next to a gasoline pump. All worked out okay.

We found an apartment in Ocean Beach, California, the drug capital of San Diego. That was okay because at the time, I was using …

We rented a two-bedroom apartment that eventually needed cleaning … wife number four said, 'This place needs deep cleaning.'

I said, 'Hire someone.'

She called a company named 'Merry Maids'. They arrived and gave us a bid that we accepted and they cleaned successfully.

That gave me the idea – I can do that and make money. When necessary, I had cleaned rooms at the motor hotel on the Cape, so I had experience.

We rented an office in a strip mall in Clairemont, part of San Diego. We put some ads for cleaning people in the newspaper as well as put door hangers in different neighborhoods for those that wanted their homes cleaned.

We had videos that showed what we expected from the employees when they were cleaning. We split the work into wet and dry work. We worked in teams of two: a captain and a mate.

I hired and did the training as well as cleaned while training.

I bid every home to make sure it was not unhealthy to clean and the homeowner was not going to mess with our staff.

Within 18 months, we were making over $8,000 a week.

The staff, to me, were more important than the customers. I could always find customers, but finding excellent staff was more difficult.

Every morning I had coffee and donuts for the staff. At Thanksgiving, I gave each a turkey, the size depending on the size of their family. At Christmas we hung stockings in the office for each employee.

We were very good.

After a cleaning, we left a stamped postcard asking 'How did we do?' My objective was to let the customers know that we cared about them.

In reference to marketing our cleaning business, we did not spend any money on advertising. What we did do is clean real estate company offices for 'FREE'. This developed into: when they had a move-in, a move-out or a clean for sale, they all called us.

Another example of this is when one real estate agency asked if we could provide staff cleaning people on Labor Day. I asked how many they needed, they said ten. I said it will cost $500 an hour. They responded – what time can you start? I paid the cleaners $25 an hour, it was a win-win.

That idea with the postcards never left my mind as to caring about others' thoughts.

In 2007, in Los Angeles, I was attending a networking luncheon. The speaker spoke about the extreme importance of following up with customers and clients. In that instant, I remembered the postcards from ten years earlier.

I signed up to use cards to develop 'The Business of Follow Up'.

We became extremely good at providing solutions to developing relationships.

In reference to keeping in contact with clients, we spend 70% of the time, energy and money on present clients, 20% on old clients and 5% on new clients.

There are many ways to keep in contact: phone, emails, texting, direct mail, greeting cards, etc. Greeting cards are the only

100% open rate, the others are between 20% and 60% effective.

There are 257 reasons to send a greeting card.

I've sent four apology cards in 13 years. One time, I took the picture of an accountant off a CEO's website as I wanted to show the CEO the power of cards. I put his picture on the front of a card with him saying, 'Nancy, we really should look at this system.' She loved the card. He was very upset. I sent another card with the picture of a person in a doghouse with the dog saying, 'Get out of my doghouse.' I apologized inside the card and sent it with 16 brownies. He now loves me.

Bottom line ... the money is in the follow-up. CARDS WORK!

ROBERT H. ROSENTHAL

PhD in Follow Up
Murrieta, Ca.

A degree in business management from FDU is only one step in Robert's stairway of success. Robert has an extensive background in customer service and customer relations as the owner of multiple hotels, restaurants and nightclubs all along the East Coast. When he moved to California, he continued his career in restaurants throughout the San Diego area, also expanding into other industries till he resigned from brick and mortar and went to click and order which he could run from home.

He is a CEO Space international certified entrepreneur, and if he's achieved anything in his decades as an entrepreneur, it's graduating from a PhD in excuses to a PhD in follow-up. He understands how implementing a solid follow-up program will bring exponential success to any business.

But he also knows there is more to it than that, and that many business owners struggle to find the information, guidance and support they need to create success.

That is why Robert co-founded MyHomeBiz.TIPS with Andrea Koochin in 2020 so that they could share their knowledge and talents with a larger audience and make a bigger impact. They have put together an outstanding leadership team of consultants, coaches and like-minded entrepreneurs who strive to aid others in their quest for business success, and the TV show is the place to meet them all and learn from them so that you too can build a prosperous business at home.

Contact: robert@phdinfollowup.com

COURAGE TO CONTINUE

JEAN MARIE RUSSO

'Success is not final; failure is not fatal; it is the courage to continue that counts.' Such profound words of wisdom from Winston Churchill.

In my mind, it begins with the courage to say 'yes'. Those are the defining moments, the teaching moments of lessons learned, the significant moments of my life which were born each time I said 'yes' to the risk. Those were the moments which complete me and identify the foundation of which I build my legacy for generations to come.

15 September 2007 1:00 pm my world changed. I knew exactly where I was. I was standing next to my father's bed, holding his hand, with my mother on his right. I bent down and asked him, 'Dad, if there was one thing you wanted us to know, what is it?'

He paused, and whispered, 'Knowledge. Knowledge is power,' and closed his eyes.

The knowledge spoken of builds our self-confidence and the

courage within us to continue.

My father's words echo in my mind even today. I embraced life taking risks, including climbing the rungs to the 30-foot ladder to the crow's nest of a yacht in my pearls and heels to admire the breathtaking view of the water. He was my mentor, who, after 42 years, retired as an enlisted officer US Air Force in communications, a morse code expert, and continued sharing his wisdom with his last breath. He was married to his soulmate, my beautiful mother, two days shy of 59 years. He had loyalty, pride, experience, but truly, knowledge and wisdom. He was significant in my son's life as his grandfather, his mentor, his coach, his 'buddy'. I take his words and legacy to heart and share them in the story that follows, in the hopes of making a difference to all who read this.

My story began on 30 April 2019, my world changed in a moment. The milestone signified my retirement and the day I said 'yes', as it was the day, I transitioned from the corporate world of 25 years to being an entrepreneur. I had an incredible career, of which I feel blessed. My entire career I commuted sometimes two-plus hours each day, I was a single parent and cared for my parents 20 of those years. Nothing could have prepared me for what I was about to experience.

Prior to walking out the door for the last time as an employee, I had one additional document to sign, a non-compete agreement. I understood immediately the purpose of the document. My heart sank. I did not plan for this. A non-compete agreement is a legal agreement in a contract specifying that an employee must not enter competition with an employer after the employment period is over. As an entrepreneur my corporation focused on global meeting and event planning, which posed a threat to the corporation I was retiring from. The agreement went into effect immediately with a duration of three years.

Beginning day one of my retirement I needed to pivot and identify a strategy for my new corporation. I took a risk in believing in me. I had competencies and I would make this work. When faced with a challenge at every turn, it took faith of the unseen. It took courage to continue. There was no way to have prepared for this moment, or to picture the future.

Knowledge is power; continuing education, achieving certifications and degrees DO matter! Case in point! I realize now I had a hidden treasure that I was unaware of it was courage and perseverance.

To share the significance and give you a visual, in 2007 there were 2.3 million entrepreneurs; December 2019 there were 31 million entrepreneurs; in December 2021 there were 528 million entrepreneurs (per a survey by The Global Entrepreneurship Monitor) according to NorthOne www.northone.com in the article: *12 Entrepreneur Statistics to Know in 2021.*

I did not plan for saturation of the entrepreneur world! No doubt, you understand. It is about the challenges we face. It could be a situation beyond your control, a loss of a job, or career change and at the ninth hour an unforeseen situation changed completely your vision and your dream.

I hear you. You are asking: 'What does one do?' Allow me to share my insights: 1) Gratitude is necessary; 2) Passion is imperative; 3) Perseverance is essential; 4) Pivoting is vital; and 5) Courage is critical.

It took courage to continue. Our life experiences make us who we are. Along with the rest of the world I experienced losing 20 family members and close friends to COVID-19 and had major life changes. Who knew we would learn to pivot together, learning the value of online presence (thank you, Heather Burgett) and the technology of Zoom and virtual meetings?

It took courage to continue, to learn the fundamentals of networking and connecting people to be my niche as it became my lifeline. The Executive Networking Events Inner Circle was a divine appointment (thank you, Tyson McIntyre and Shelly Yorgesen, CEO of ENE Inner Circle). My world and my inner circle grew and evolved. The value: Priceless.

It took courage to continue. Failure was not an option, despite the loneliness. I learned not be hard on those individuals who did not understand me or my business. I learned to be understanding and not to judge them. What I was embarking upon is difficult for others to comprehend. I knew to be forgiving.

It takes courage to learn and understand people have a different mindset and see failure; they want to believe you; however, they are not capable. The achievement of success has delays that are out of your control. The delays are viewed as 'excuses' and thus your credibility and reputation are at stake. It took courage and faith of the unseen.

I share my pearls of wisdom in how to reap the rewards: 1) Always take the adventure; do not give in to fear; 3) Ask forgiveness, not permission; 4) Doing nothing is not an option; and 5) It takes courage to builds inner strength, courage to continue.

Know you have already achieved success before the journey even begins when you say 'yes'. Know this is about you; your handprint and your legacy for generations to come.

In the words of Paul Harvey ... 'And the rest of the story ...'

20 December 2021, I was honored with being honoree recipient of the 2021 BRAINZ Global 500 List of Entrepreneurs and Influential Leaders; I publicly thank BRAINZ Global. From a

business perspective one would think this was the reward: but no, there was more …

Yes, I was without words, humbled and honored just three years into my journey because I said 'yes' to be included amongst such a list with prestigious, incredible individuals and global influential leaders, including empowering iconic people such as Oprah and Karen McDermott.

The reward came because I found the courage to say 'yes' to being an entrepreneur. It opened doors, allowed me to meet incredible people, and enduring friends of the heart. This honor was about embracing the people I met, elevating them, their business and their platform, connecting people to make a difference. It was about the experiences, the adventures, lessons learned and wisdom gained through which it provides one with knowledge building inner strength and courage.

The defining moments, the teaching moments of lessons learned, the significant moments of my life were born each time I said 'yes' to the risk. Those were the moments which completed me and the foundation of which I build my legacy for generations to come.

Failure is not an option; it is an opportunity and sometimes you must be the one to create that opportunity. Take the risk; look within and find the courage to continue. Truly, in my mind, *The Art of Risk and Reward* begins with the courage to say 'yes' and the courage to continue what counts.

Gratitude of the heart, Winston Churchill, for your words of wisdom: *'Success is not final; failure is not fatal; it is the courage to continue that counts.'*

JEAN MARIE RUSSO

Speaking of Success, Inc.
Kenosha, Wisconsin.

After 25+ years with billion-dollar fortune 100 corporations, Jean Marie took early retirement and became an entrepreneur as a consultant, global speaker and influencer of Speaking of Success, Inc., a high-profile, international speakers bureau, focusing on global speaking, executive coaching and consulting, training, webinars, mastermind classes, podcasts and summits. Jean Marie was an Honoree Recipient of the 2021 BRAINZ Global 500 List of Entrepreneurs and Influential Leaders Award.

Jean Marie is primarily a proud mother and mother-in-law to her amazing son and beautiful, intelligent daughter-in-law; and an exceptionally proud and fun Nana of three incredible, bright, cheeky grandsons whom she loves to the moon and back. She is an author, a previous global radio personality, international speaker and pre-eminent business strategist coach and consultant.

Jean Marie is a protégé of Christopher Kai, one of the world's top professional gifted speakers and is a member of his gifted professional speakers program. She holds a business, PR, executive, medical and legal administration degree and a class A certification in modeling, Milwaukee, WI, along with a paralegal certification from Carthage College, Kenosha, WI.

Jean Marie is a member of the Executive Networking Events (ENE) Inner Circle and has been invited to be an American delegate for the sixth annual conference of American entrepreneurs, Oxford University, Oxford, England. She has served as a member on the board of directors of the Domestic Violence Project, a board member of the Women's Life Insurance Society for the local chapter in Wisconsin. She is an active advisory board member for Sign World Studios, Inc., CEO, producer and deaf Emmy Award-winning actor, CJ Jones, who is one of her high-profile global influencers and speakers and is starring in *Avatar 2;* he is also the creator of the Na'vi sign language for *Avatar 2.*

Jean Marie is an expert connector of her global speakers and individuals with agencies, organizations, corporations, associations and angel investors with her high-profile global influencers and professional speakers, such as Christopher Kai, one of the top world professional speakers; and Heather Burgett of the award-winning PR Firm, The Burgett Group.

Jean Marie's Mantra: 'It's about people making a difference.'

Contact: speakingofsuccessinc@gmail.com

TOXIC WORKPLACE TO POST TRAUMATIC GROWTH
BLACKLISTED DURING THE PANDEMIC TO STARTING MY OWN BUSINESS!

JULIA GOLD

Success is the best revenge.

I am Julia Gold and I own a leadership consulting and executive coaching business.

Owning this business allows me to work with amazing professionals and executives around the world. I am a catalyst and guide that helps them with leadership challenges and shaping an intentional culture. During the pandemic, millions of people re-evaluated how they were spending their time in a finite day, week and life. Many decided to restructure how many hours a week they work, where they work from and the type of work that brings them joy, purpose and satisfaction. I help with career confusion, paralysis and transitions. I help high-performance professionals connect with the values that are important to them and match that with an industry, company or start their own entrepreneurship journey.

By the time you are reading this, I will be hosting an international adventure leadership retreat focusing on activities that parallel and bring out emotions that we can harness and lessons we can learn. One of those lessons is breaking through fear and limitations we have placed on ourselves. During adventure retreats, we will be immersed in situations where we have to adapt quickly, problem-solve and make decisions! Those lessons translate to our business and our workplace and the leaders we can become.

My mission and goal is to make an impact and change workplace culture. We are at the tipping point of a societal shift in acknowledging and changing toxic workplaces. Toxic workplaces affect mental health and can cause health effects such as: overwhelm, burnout, fatigue, depression, anxiety, PTSD and increased physical illness. Workplace effects: environment of fear, absenteeism, decreased productivity, frequent turnover, low morale, high economic costs, high conflict, gossip, favoritism and chaos. Career effects: loss of confidence in your expertise, being fired, being blacklisted, unable to get work due to malicious rumors, financial distress, housing insecurity and food insecurity.

I am raising the voices of successful professionals who have never shared their toxic workplace experiences through my podcast.

I host strategic leadership calls with owners and executives. During these calls, breakthroughs are made such as changing the type of business that will be launched or the direction of the company.

I wake up energized and excited to work with clients and companies in an area I feel strongly aligned with.

However, my journey to get here was difficult and full of challenges. I was in multiple toxic workplaces, one after another, asking myself why I kept ending up there. I packed up my car and drove across the country to help start a crisis center in a rural location. While working as a first responder making sure no-one was in danger, I also had to come back to an office culture of rumors, screaming, crying and manipulation by so-called leaders. I was targeted for standing up to unethical behavior and for providing support to my team members. Meanwhile, I provided clinical support, dealt with questions from the community, did outreach and coordinated everyone's work schedules.

Finally, I was about to leave on a volunteer trip abroad that had been requested and approved almost a year in advance. I was called into the office and told that it was too long and I would have to take a leave of absence and then reapply for the position. I saw through this attempt to get rid of me, and also the opportunity to leave this unhealthy and toxic workplace. I gladly left without a backwards glance. I reflected on how important it was to have a supportive leadership structure and workplace especially when providing vital life-and-death services on little sleep.

My next job I was supervising multiple crisis teams out in the field. Before my first day, I was warned of a toxic individual with unethical behavior that was aggressive towards a previous co-worker. Soon after I started, his egotistical and manipulative behavior became apparent. I had several staff members complain of bullying, harassment and fear causing them to want to quit. He caused issues towards the goals of the team and organization. However, the issues ran deeper. His supervisor would cover for him and get the whole department to try to gaslight me, record conversations and try to undermine me. Once again, the individuals we serve would suffer. I walked out, resignation effective immediately, after one of the top members of an organization launched a campaign to smear my reputation. He did this to cover up unethical and sexist behavior by one of his subordinates. So I walked out, as I do not compromise my ethics or values.

I had no income and no savings when I walked out. I was blacklisted and unable to get another job in the industry. The 'leaders' from both organizations made sure to spread lies and rumors about me to jobs in the state that I had applied to.

As I processed what had occurred and my next step, I realized this experience can open up the space for other things to be in my life. I keep my values front and center: ethics, helping others, standing up for what is right, refusing to back down in the face of bullying, toxic leadership and sexism. I have a drive to succeed and excel despite the naysayers.

These experiences caused a hit to my confidence, caused me to question my career path, all while hustling to keep a roof over my head and food on the table through doing odd jobs. It took therapy, processing and professional development, and realizing the main things I took away from these experiences are the horrible effects on professionals in these situations. I remembered my staff and co-workers exposed to this toxicity while working physically and mentally demanding jobs. So I decided to do something about it!

When I was brainstorming how to launch my business, many people, including family, told me not to take the risk and kept asking me if I was making money from the time I was putting into the set-up. That thinking is not strategic as you have to have an eagle's-eye view of the future and how what you create will have the impact you seek! I knew that my training and experiences aligned with my passion to change workplaces into positive, productive and intentional places. I also wanted to help professionals recover from toxic workplaces and break through to the career of their dreams.

I am about to launch my 'Toxic Workplace Recovery' course. Recovering from a toxic work environment (mailchi.mp).

Now I am excited to jump into the unknown again by focusing full-time on expanding services and growing my company.

JULIA GOLD

Hopeful Bluebird Consulting, LLC
Colorado.

Julia Gold LPC, LCADC is a psychotherapist and supervisor who has over 15 years' experience working with individuals and businesses in crisis. She is the owner and founder of Hopeful Bluebird Consulting, LLC and currently helps executives and entrepreneurs recover from toxic workplaces, career paralysis and imposter syndrome. She works with organizations to create a positive work culture, diversity and inclusion, burnout prevention and de-escalation strategies.

Julia has a unique style of blending her academic experience with her life experience and acts as a catalyst for executives to go from career paralysis to career success.

Julia works as a disrupter and change agent within organizational systems with high chaos and conflict transform to cohesion. Julia has traveled to over 50 countries and uses her expertise to transform adventure travel experiences to enhance leadership skills.

Contact: Hopefulbluebird7@gmail.com

CHANGING LIVES WITH THE HELP OF A STRANGER

TOBIE SPEARS

When I became a mother, I counted how many summers I got to spend with my girls before they found their wings and left the safety of my home. In retrospect, now that they are nearly grown, I felt like we had so much more time. I knew that my days with them in my home were limited, and I wanted all the time we could squeeze out of their childhoods to be full of adventures. In 2012, according to my calculations, I had nine summers left with Justice and 13 with Trinity. I had dreamed of an experience that would bring our family closer when we made the life-changing decision to spend three months living in the developing nation of Guatemala. Justice was ten and Trinity was six years old.

Risking it all, we rented out our home in Utah, packed all our belongings, left our friends and family, and drove off towards a country full of unknowns. My husband Darrin, Justice, Trinity and I loaded our car and drove 2,826 miles over 12 days from Utah to a little town in Guatemala. This trip inevitably changed my family forever. What I thought was going to be a few months living in a developing country turned out to be a lifelong love for the country and the people I could never have expected.

While in Guatemala, I taught English while my girls attended school at the same campus, and Darrin was volunteering as a nurse. On the weekends, we'd plan outings so that we could see more of the country. One weekend we volunteered at an orphanage in the highlands of Solola. My daughters loved the children, reading to them, snuggling with them and feeding them while Darrin did physicals, and I provided over 50 haircuts. We worked most of the day, laughing with and showing love to these kiddos. We also cried as we learned how many of these children had come to live in this orphanage.

International adoptions were not allowed, so many children would live out their lives without being adopted into a forever family. My young daughters got to experience what life is like inside an orphanage. They also got to learn one of my fundamental beliefs, that we can all give love. We can show love to children who speak another language, infants who don't yet talk, people with different customs and cultures, and children with varying skin colors. This invaluable lesson was made available to our kids because of our humanitarian travel.

In May of 2012, we wrote to our family back home, 'We are doing good. We are still settling in. It took us two days to find hangers and several different trips to several stores. We live in a middle-class, gated community in a 400 sq ft home, with a pila (an outside cement sink) we use to wash our clothes and our dishes. We're still figuring all that out. The days of loading a dishwasher or washing machine are gone for a while. The comforts of "home" are so much more appreciated! There are no closets, cupboards or countertops. We ordered a table to be made so that we can use it for preparing our meals. They had to make it specifically for people who are at least six inches taller than most locals. Our girls have been AMAZING!! They have not once said a negative word about anything. They volunteer to wash our clothes and have been great helpers mopping, sweeping and unpacking. We have sprayed the entire place several times for the cockoaches, flies or red wasps :) Gratefully the only roaches we've found were dead!! Still adjusting to all of the critters, though :) Know that we send our love from Guatemala.'

I have always liked to travel like a local. When we are in Mexico, Guatemala or Belize, our family rents a home in a local neighborhood to understand what it's like to experience that community. When many of us vacation, we fly into another country, take a taxi to a resort and spend a blissful week soaking in the sun. When friends ask, we tell them we loved the country and encourage them to go. There is wonder in an all-inclusive resort, however, I want to see how life is lived in another country.

In 2012 Guatemala had no wi-fi, no smartphones and the country had no GPS. Darrin and I used a paper map to get us through much of Mexico and Guatemala. If ever we were lost, we would ask someone the way, and they would kindly tell us we had 15 more minutes. Often those 15 minutes turned out to be several hours, but now anytime the girls ask us how much longer, they might hear the reply, 'Just 15 minutes more.'

In 2020, Guatemala and the rest of the world was shut down due to COVID-19. People were stuck in their homes without food and no possibility of work. Families in Guatemala put out white flags on their front door letting neighbors know that the family inside was out of food.

I was sending money to Guatemalan friends and organizations

that were able to buy food and deliver it to their neighborhoods. It was simply the only thing I could think of. We were all struck with such fear. After seeing posts about the food distribution, a woman named Linda reached out to me on social media asking me for money. What was different about her was she was asking me if we could help her feed the hungry people in her community. My initial reaction was to say no. I am not in the habit of giving hundreds of dollars to someone I've never met. I told her I would need two days to think about this arrangement. I had looked for someone that lived in Guatemala and would work as hard as I do to help the people there. I had wanted to meet someone like Linda for years and I was thrilled that she might be 'the one'. I decided to send her $600. With $600 Linda and her husband were able to feed 53 families for 30 days. For about $20 a family, Linda made sure that hundreds of people were fed. I was elated.

After getting to know Linda, she shared with me that she wanted to start a preschool. The schools were closed and she had just lost her teaching job. She was now home with her small children and wanted to be teaching other children. I explained to her my desire to start a nutrition center that would work hand in hand helping children grow healthy bodies and brains. Because Guatemala ranks about the fourth most malnourished country in the world it didn't make sense to only provide an educational opportunity.

Linda and I decided that we could do both, and without any sponsors we started our breakfast program bringing kiddos a warm breakfast five days a week. As sponsors signed up, we were able to add preschool and then lunch to our day, and with a generous grant, we were able to add dinner boxes to our week. We are currently providing thousands of meals a month to our community and are in the process of buying land to build a sewing center. We are making huge strides and I am elated to see the changes in our community. I took a risk on Linda and it has paid off. I believe in creating win-win experiences and I believe that is what we create with the volunteers who join us and the people we serve in Guatemala.

Being brave enough to leave our comfort zone opened up our lives to lifelong friendships and connections. I simply can't imagine what my life would look like if Guatemala wasn't in it. I would certainly have more free time and our family would certainly have more money, but we would have missed out on nine years of incredible memories made. Together we have swam with whale sharks, watched dolphins play in the ocean over breakfast, ridden horseback up an active volcano, donated thousands of backpacks full of school supplies, watched butterflies migrate, enjoyed new foods, hiked Mayan ruins, filled libraries with books, volunteered, fallen, thrown up, froze in short cold showers, cut each other's hair, become creative, made new friends and loved each other a lot.

I believe that we get more out of giving. I believe that we needed these experiences for our souls to grow, and I am grateful that I could create these memories with my daughters. We are all part of making a difference collectively in this world simply by opening our hearts and working together to create change. We all have the ability to embody what we would like to see reflected in the world by sharing love, kindness and compassion. We rise when we lift others up! I am blessed to know many kind-hearted individuals who make this world a better place and I encourage you to join us.

Please contact me if you are interested in volunteering in Guatemala, sponsoring a kiddo or donating to our preschool, our nutrition program or our sewing center.

Thank you so much,

Tobie Spears founder/director Be Humanitarian

TOBIE SPEARS

Be Humanitarian
Pleasant Grove, UT USA

Tobie Spears graduated from the University of Utah with degrees in sociology and political science and a certificate in criminology. She is lucky enough to have an awesome husband of 25 years, two amazing daughters and three crazy cats.

Tobie fell in love with traveling as a teenager when she backpacked through Europe and drove cross-country with her best friends. After college she started traveling with her husband and daughters, and in 2013, they drove from Utah to Guatemala where they lived, worked and volunteered for three months. Tobie stays busy running her non-profit organization, Be Humanitarian, where she leads 11-day tours exploring Guatemala, giving back and having a blast. Her volunteer-run nutrition program is providing thousands of meals a month and her volunteer-run preschool is offering educational support to children, teens and parents in a remote Guatemalan community. Tobie's community is working together to fight childhood malnutrition through education and nutrition, and you are welcome to join her.

Contact: support@behumanitarian.org

PEACE CAN BE FOUND

JORDELLE LOVELL

I sat looking at God's beauty in front of me. Rolling hills covered in farm fields, evergreen trees situated ever so perfectly on the mountains that surround our valley. As I looked up at the blue sky and fluffy clouds painted in the sky above me, I watched a flock of geese fly away. Jim's snort brought me back to reality as I reminisced on why I was here. But oh, that peace. I didn't want to leave it. I closed my eyes and breathed out again, crying in relief at the peace of mind just found.

We all take risks in life based on our gut. We also don't make the best decisions or take the best risks based on not listening to our gut. My story comes from a risk I took recently that resulted in a reward I wasn't expecting.

Two years ago, I was an emotional mess. I was coming from a broken-down moment in my life where I found myself wanting to build a strong foundation. I wanted to say 'NO' to those toxic people and relationships that were eating me up. So, I dug up an old love of mine to put me on the right path. A love I'd had since my childhood: my love for horses. They brought me so much joy in my younger life, so I banked on them to help me heal once again.

It was a warm summer day, the kids and I were at the family cabin nestled up in the beautiful hills by the Snake River, in Idaho. We had our sweet horse, Jim, a tall and loving horse that looks like Spirit from the TV series. The kids had finished their turns and I was ready to jump on and go.

After swinging up on the saddle, I gave him a little cluck and off we went. He moved forward and as I let the reins loose, he took the cue to go faster. He took the hill like it was nothing. We came to the top of the hill at a speed I can't even begin to explain. He was moving so fast it was as if nothing was under me. It felt incredible. It was as if I was flying with eagles and soaring with the breeze. It was then and there I felt free – free from all the cares, the struggles, the worries, the insecurities and negative people in my life. I let those tears of frustration and self-doubt roll down my cheeks as we ran at the highest possible speed Jim could muster. I left those insecurities in the dust and didn't look back. I took a step in the right direction for myself that day. I let those nasty thoughts, fears, self-doubts and terrible people go. No longer would I be their slave.

As we came trotting back down the hill to the kids, I knew I had taken a step in the right direction. I was ready to build on it.

A few months later, I decided I was ready to take on a challenge, expand my abilities a bit. I bought an older mare, a girl, that had never been ridden. In the horse world you typically 'break' a horse between the ages of two and six, my girl was around 11. But something in my gut said to do it, and so I did! I learned how to work my mare safely and confidently on the ground, in a round pen. It wasn't all sunshine and rainbows. We had many things get in the way. She fractured her cannon bone in two places. There were expensive vet bills, I got hurt on more than one occasion, and she had bad habits developed from never being ridden as a young horse. I watched hours of training videos, asked for guidance from my horse-smart sister and friends. Then one day, my husband came out after I had saddled her up and said, 'Let's do it! You're ready, she's ready, jump on.'

So, I did!

I couldn't believe it, I took a huge leap of faith in myself that day. A risk with an unknown outcome. This ride could have gone very western. But I jumped on, I took a horse that had never been ridden and swung on up! She stood like a champ and we walked forward with no kicking! I took myself from the average pleasure-riding cowgirl, to learning how to gain respect, train, correct and notice things in my horses. I went from having one horse to having six. I felt like I was finding my new place in training horses. I was happier, I was more confident, I was doing me in my world and I felt successful.

But this story isn't over yet.

The respect I was earning in the round pen with my horses was giving me permission to take control of my personal life. I felt okay about saying, 'No, you're not for me.' I was ending toxic relationships all while finding a healthy balance in myself. This risk I took on myself certainly seemed to be paying off.

I learned over the next two years of horse work that I needed this journey with my project horses more than I needed them. So, I found my project horses beautiful new homes, then asked myself what I was ready for next.

I felt like I was ready to invest in a well-trained horse. The years of training I had put myself through not only taught me about how to really ride and take care of my horses, but also helped me feel ready for a younger, stronger and more confident horse. This was a big deal! I had never spent big money on a horse before – but I was ready.

I kept my eyes open in all the social groups I was in and the online listings sites in our area. Then one day, I found him! A big beautiful black and white Gypsy Vanner horse. He was the right age, he was beautiful, he had the right mannerisms, and he was 'bombproof!' He was perfect.

We reviewed the seller's website, looked over the pictures, read the reviews, the story seemed to check out and so on. We had been given an address that we googled to show a horse property. Everything seemed legit. But there was this gut feeling from the very beginning saying this was too good to be true. I brushed the feeling aside as a negative thought and proceeded forward anyway.

We were approved for our adoption of Fin rather quickly, then asked to put half the money down through a 'cash banking' app to reserve him. Being nervous, my hubs and I looked everything over one more time, and even spoke to the 'owner' on the phone before sending the money over. The horse was ten hours away, and we wanted to secure him. So, we sent over half the payment, then agreed to have him delivered to us for another set amount of money that I sent. It all seemed perfect – yup, too perfect.

One week later, my sister-in-law and I, who was also trying to purchase two of his horses, went to pick up my dream horse Fin. After driving five hours, we stopped at a friend's house for the night. That's when everything began to unravel. The seller claimed to be in another state rescuing horses, and wasn't available for pick-up the next morning. He said he was never going to be available that weekend and just kept back-pedaling. We were livid.

We got in contact with the law enforcement the next morning. The deputy visited the property and confirmed our fears – we were scammed. The sweet couple living there had one family horse but had never heard of or seen the man or his horses before. Our money gone forever, the horse that I fell in love with through pictures and childish dreams, never to be mine.

An expensive risk for me to take. An expensive outcome that not only cost me a lot of hard-earned money but cost me a lot of pride too. I ugly-cried many nights. Many days I beat myself up for being foolish enough to fall for the whole con. I hated myself some days. We weren't cash rich and for me to lose that amount was devastating for me. My husband was so great to never blame and only comfort and forgive me. My kids were open armed and caring. I was truly surrounded by love, but still truly hurt. I had to do something.

So I went to work. I spent days on the phone with my bank, the cash app help desk, the bank the money was transferred to and did everything possible we could do with the authorities. We never got our money back. Everyone told us the same thing, 'Sorry.'

Weeks later we learned the seller lives in India and stole pictures and reviews from other horse people. I was devastated. However, after doing everything I could with the proper channels, I felt like there was still something else I could do. I knew I had an audience online that would hear my story. As hard as it was to open up to the world, I took to my social platform and spilled my guts. I was shaking before I hit the 'post' button, knowing how vulnerable this would make me. I needed to try and help others though, so I pushed the big blue 'post' button.

I told people the risk I had taken in putting money down on a horse I hadn't seen and how terribly it turned out for me. I advised them to be wise in their online purchases and asked for help in blocking the scammer. Many were sympathetic and others were blunt in their 'Yah, I saw that scam from a mile away.' But as awful as some comments were, I was reminded of the many, many good people in my corner cheering me on while I was down on my knees in a vulnerable space.

An inner motivation slowly bubbled up inside me weeks after the scam took place. It reminded me how invincible I felt on my horse Jim that summer day, running across those hills. It told me that I would ride harder and ride better because that's who I am. I will be better from this!

'Take risks: if you win, you will be happy. If you lose, you will be wise.' – Author unknown

I will one day find another horse to replace the part of me that I lost. Until then I am going to sit atop my beautiful Jim and enjoy the sun warming my face. I am going to bask in the peaceful feeling that is telling me that I really am wiser every day, because I am learning to be open and to learn from my mistakes. And that is reward enough for me.

Now you know the rest of my story, for now.

JORDELLE LOVELL

JL Design & Video
Ririe, ID USA

Jordelle Lovell is the founder of JL Design & Video, a graphic designer who enjoys putting together logos, PPTs, social media graphics/ads, printables and swag. She has successfully directed and organized events at the local school, church and community levels. She also has successfully planned networking events not only close to home but also at Crom Castle, in Northern Ireland. Jordelle is also a bestselling author and lover of her husband, four children, family and her fur babies – yes, her horses. When she isn't outside riding or tuning up her horses, you can find her volunteering as president of the parent teacher student organization at her children's school and coaching their sport teams throughout the school year.

Contact: jordellelovell@gmail.com